A FILM LOVER'S GUIDE TO SANTA FE

a FILM LOVER'S GUIDE to SANTA FE

University of New Mexico Press

Albuquerque

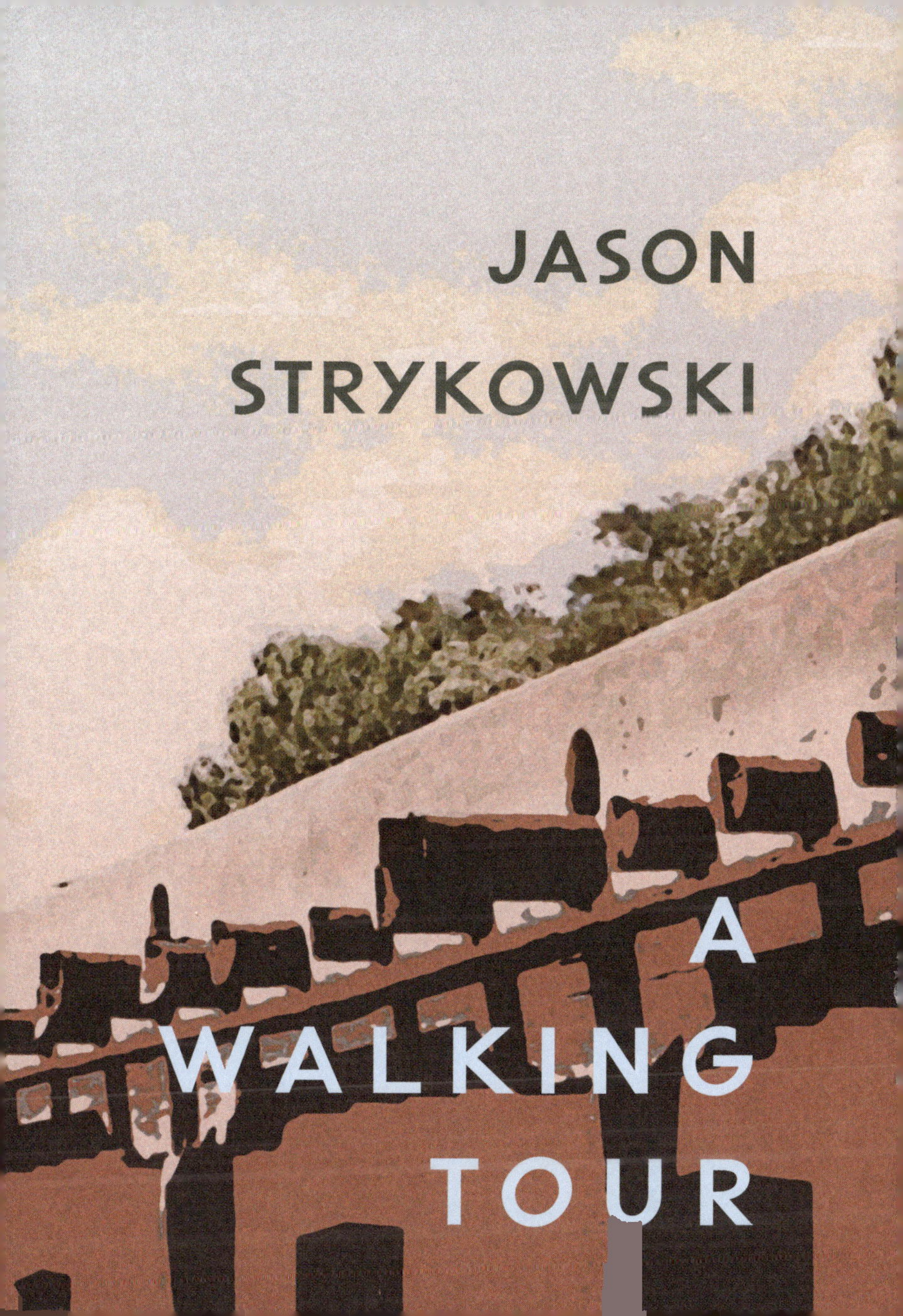
JASON
STRYKOWSKI
A
WALKING
TOUR

Printed in the United States of America

ISBN 978-0-8263-6929-1 (paper)
ISBN 978-0-8263-6930-7 (ePub)

Library of Congress Control Number: 2025945351

Founded in 1889, the University of New Mexico sits on the traditional homelands of the Pueblo of Sandia. The original peoples of New Mexico—Pueblo, Navajo, and Apache—since time immemorial have deep connections to the land and have made significant contributions to the broader community statewide. We honor the land itself and those who remain stewards of this land throughout the generations and also acknowledge our committed relationship to Indigenous peoples. We gratefully recognize our history.

Cover illustration adapted from image via Wikimedia Commons
Designed by Isaac Morris
Composed in Arno Pro, Gill Sans, and Sharktooth

Contents

Part I. Walking Tours

Part II. Driving Tours

Introduction

As I sit down to write this book, hundreds of film production workers swarm through the small motel where I have hung my hat and dropped my bags. The crew has repainted a wing of the motel. Then they replaced the interior of a room, just feet away from mine, with their own furnishings. And they've placed electrical cords throughout the building. It takes me a little bit of effort to make sure I don't trip over them while heading back to my room.

Although I spent years working on films and television shows in New Mexico, my current employers are in different states, and I have little to do with productions inside the Land of Enchantment. Yet I can't escape them. Film crews are everywhere in Santa Fe. Turn any corner and you might find the latest prestige show for a streaming service, Hollywood blockbuster, or low-budget indie. It's all here.

Centuries of art and cultural heritage are here too.

Long the capital of Spanish, Mexican, and American New Mexico, Santa Fe is the hub of everything Southwest. Within the city limits are around 250 fine art galleries, museums, and restaurants all purveying the finest foods and arts the region has to offer. Many of these attractions are housed in buildings that have stood the test of time for hundreds of years. The city is also home to several art festivals that attract around 100,000 annually. The most famous of these, the Southwestern Association for Indian Arts Santa Fe Indian Market, held every summer, is the preeminent gathering of its kind in the United States. Native American art from this event finds its way to galleries and museums all over the world.

The same can be said of the many films and television shows that shoot here. They all start in Santa Fe and wind up on screens across the world. Little Santa Fe has a gargantuan footprint.

It also has confusing streets, sidewalks, and trails. Ancient roads once built for horses, burros, and carriages still wind lazily through town. Getting lost is easy. In fact, I recommend it. But before you wander into a historical plaza, a highly regarded museum, or a hidden restaurant, use the walking and driving tours in the following pages to give you a basic orientation and introduce you to filming locations and important cultural and historical sites throughout the City Different. Just make sure to look up on occasion—odds are pretty good you'll walk directly into an active television set. Try not to trip on the electrical cords.

Welcome to Santa Fe

Writer/director Scott Cooper introduced Santa Fe in an early draft of his screenplay for the independent drama *Crazy Heart* (2009), based on the novel of the same name by Thomas Cobb. In the scene, Bad Blake, played by Jeff Bridges, checks the place out:

```
EXT. ESTABLISHING—SANTA FE, NEW MEXICO—DAY
The buildings are low and nestled in the hills. It's
flat as hell . . .

EXT. STREETS OF SANTA FE—AFTERNOON
Bad walks through the middle of town. The streets of
Santa Fe are narrow and lined with art galleries.
Out on the sidewalk, Indians display their jewelry,
baskets, and trinkets on blankets.
```

Here, Cooper, who also directed *Hostiles* (2017) and *Out of the Furnace* (2013), showed the keen eye and powers of observation that would ultimately net him an Academy Award. He also previewed a grudging appreciation of Santa Fe that permeated his film. Santa Fe's personality shone through in *Crazy Heart,* as it had many films before. The city has inspired and charmed filmmakers, artists, and tourists for more than a century.

Below the Sangre de Cristo Mountains and along the banks of the Santa Fe River, Santa Fe is naturally scenic. Pine trees and aspens turn the mountain slopes bright green in the spring and summer and yellow in the fall. Cottonwood, pinion, and juniper dot the muted brown of the mesas and valleys with intermittent flashes of color. Low adobe buildings, many with a Pueblo Revival or Territorial style (more on these aesthetics later), spread from the foothills toward the desert. They're punctuated

by a stone cathedral just feet from the Santa Fe Plaza, the city's historic center.

At the southern tip of the Rockies, the greater Santa Fe area is temperate, with more than 300 sunny days each year. Highs rarely cross above 100 degrees Fahrenheit and lows rarely below 20. In the late summer and early fall, seasonal rains, locally referred to as monsoons, keep the dust and heat down. It is, however, prone to fast changes in weather and direct sunlight, thanks to the elevation (more on preparing for that later). Often confused with the Sonoran Desert of Arizona, New Mexico is actually a "high desert" and not prone to the same extreme temperatures as its neighboring state. You also won't find a single saguaro cactus near Santa Fe.

Those same conditions have made the area a desirable place to call home for thousands of years. Ancestral Puebloans—the forebears of today's Puebloan peoples—built permanent villages along the Santa Fe River beginning sometime around 850 BCE, although hunter-gatherers set up camp in the area seasonally for many years prior to that. These early Santa Feans farmed corn, beans, and squash. They made pottery and lived in adobe-style homes. Their communities grew larger and more developed until the 1400s, when a drought forced them to move to other inhabited areas.

Two centuries later, Santa Fe was little more than a temporary camp for travelers. That changed in 1610, when Don Pedro de Peralta chose to make it the second capital of Spanish New Mexico. He named it Villa Real de la Santa Fé de San Francisco de Asis, roughly meaning "Royal City of the Holy Faith of St. Francis of Assisi." It didn't take long for the name to be

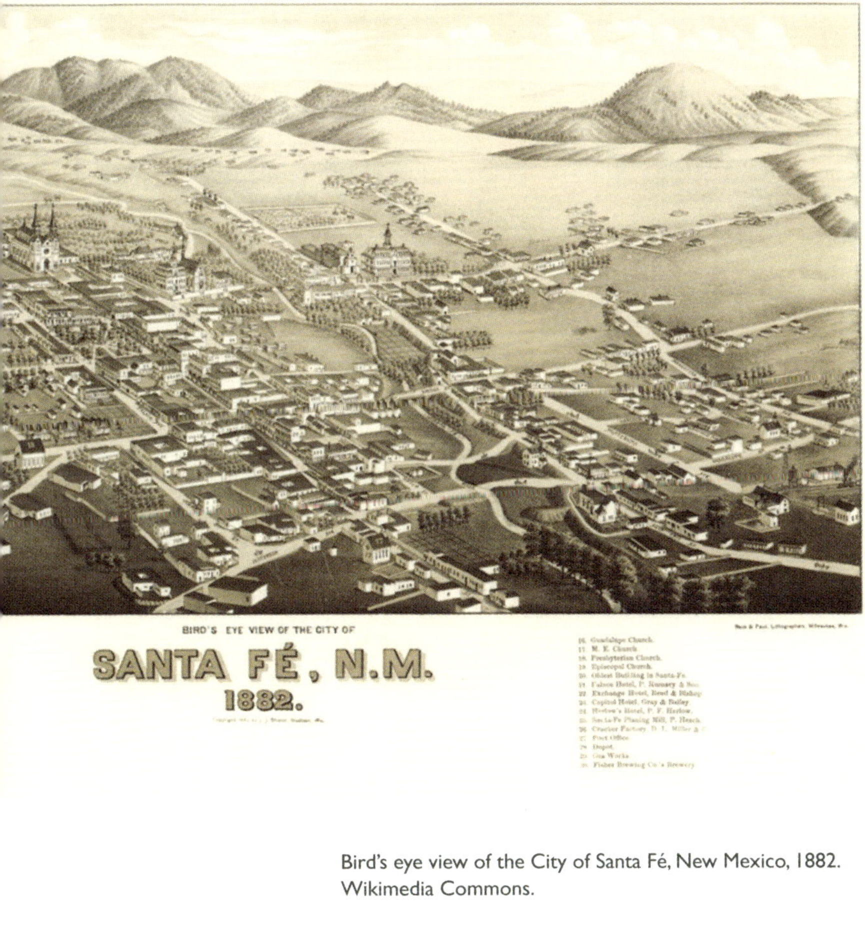

Bird's eye view of the City of Santa Fé, New Mexico, 1882.
Wikimedia Commons.

unofficially shortened to Santa Fe. Although, in some ways, the city maintains its faithful nature. In addition to bestowing the settlement with a name, Spanish colonists constructed a secure plaza in the area and a fort. They also built a seat of government that would be referred to as to the Palace of the Governors. (105 West Palace Ave, Santa Fe, NM, 87501; 505-476-5100, nmhistorymuseum.org). More on that building and the attached museum can be found in the Page to Screen tour (page 4).

After decades of Spanish dominion, New Mexico's Puebloan peoples successfully overthrew the colonial regime in 1680, with the Pueblo Revolt. Exhausted of their inability to practice ancestral religion under the mission system, the Puebloan peoples organized their revolt under the leadership of Po'pay, who is now memorialized in marble in the National Statuary Hall in Washington, DC. For more than a decade, Puebloan peoples enjoyed the freedom to practice their ancestral religion without interference from Spanish missionaries until the Spanish returned in 1692 and regained control, which they held for more than a century.

In 1821, following Mexico's independence from Spain, Santa Fe and all of Nueva España became Mexican property. Under Mexican governance, Santa Fe transformed into a central trading terminus along a trail that bore the city's name. The famed path ran some 800 miles from Independence, Missouri, to Santa Fe and saw the frequent exchange of manufactured goods for furs. This oft-romanticized period was short-lived and faded away after the United States took Santa Fe following the conclusion of the Mexican-American War that ended in 1848 with the Treaty of Guadalupe Hidalgo. The city itself slowly morphed into a different shape as construction sprawled away from the Spanish plaza.

The next major change for the old capital city arrived in 1880, with the Atchison, Topeka and Santa Fe Railway. The train made Santa Fe much more accessible and a new destination for tourists interested in finding the "exotic" close to home. Eventually, Santa Fe architects came around to the tourists' desires. The city was once marked by a blend of Territorial architecture and Pueblo-style structures. Many of these were replaced, or mudded over, to more closely resemble the Pueblo Revival architecture that emerged in the decades after the tourist trade captured Santa Fe. Architects like John Gaw Meem and Mary Colter were practitioners of the style.

Santa Fe even adopted a new moniker to harness the growing interest in the city as a tourist destination. In the early 1900s, the small town took the nickname "the City Different" as part of a campaign to push its reputation as a place for art and atypical architecture. The name stuck.

The old Santa Fe Plaza became an ideal center for the new tourist trade. The small park was the perfect host for the Santa Fe Indian Market (swaia.org) that is held every year in August. Founded in 1922, the market has grown into the largest event of its kind in the world. More than 1,000 juried artists from tribes all over the country attend the event and compete for a multitude of prizes. There's also a fashion show and a grand gala. At least 100,000 people attend the event every year, filling small Santa Fe almost to the brink. If the market is on your agenda, make sure to book a hotel room early.

Tourism aside, Santa Fe is also the center of New Mexico's politics, as it has been for more than 400 years. The Palace of the Governors remained the seat of government until after the Mexican period. The territory and state government moved several times until they took up permanent residence in "the Roundhouse," New Mexico's state capitol building and current seat of government. The building is one of a few state capitols constructed with a circular footprint. The design is meant to mimic a kiva—an ancient center of worship and community used by Puebloan peoples. (More on the Roundhouse in the Page to Screen tour on page 4.)

Santa Fe Orientation

The City Different's historic center, where most of its attractions and historic charm are located, is ringed by Paseo de Peralta, named after Pedro de Peralta, a Spanish emissary who established the city and briefly served as the territorial governor. The open loop road is sealed by Guadalupe on the west and bisected by Alameda Street running east to west. The Sangre de Cristo Mountains make a handy geographic marker on the east side.

A few distinct neighborhoods cluster around downtown. The South Capitol neighborhood is not named idly and can be found close to the state's capitol. It's largely residential with a smattering of big box grocery stores. North of the capitol, you'll find two distinct older districts: Acequia Madre and Canyon Road. You can find more on Canyon Road in the Santa Funky tour on page 56. This ancient thoroughfare is the preeminent gathering of art galleries in the Southwest. Just a block away are older homes near a small aqueduct known as the Acequia Madre, which was once an essential water delivery system for the city.

Farther from the state capitol, the Railyard is one of the hippest and fastest-growing areas of the city. In addition to functional trains, you'll find breweries, theaters, and retail stores in this area. For more on the Railyard, check out the Page to Screen tour. The nearby Guadalupe District was settled as a farming district after the 1692 Reconquest and then grew more rapidly two centuries later when the railroad arrived. Single-story homes packed tightly to the street give the district its cozy and antique feel.

From its historic center, Santa Fe mostly spreads south along Cerrillos Road, which is where almost all of the city's modern retailers and services can be found. Near the southern end of town, Cerrillos crosses under Interstate 25 and turns into the Turquoise Trail.

Interstate 25 is the primary thoroughfare to Albuquerque, a drive that takes about an hour. In addition to accessing it via Cerrillos Road,

Shopping for supplies in *No Country for Old Men* (2007). Courtesy of Miramax.

The Coen Brothers in New Mexico

Born and raised in Minnesota, the writer/directors Ethan and Joel Coen have left an indelible mark in New Mexico by directing three of the best films ever produced in the state. Two could be counted as classic Westerns that played with the conventions of the genre, while the third updated the Western into a modern milieu.

The Coens broke in by writing and directing the 1984 modern noir *Blood Simple*. The film starred Frances McDormand, who became a frequent collaborator and also Joel's wife. The duo followed up with the comedy *Raising Arizona* in 1987. In the 1990s, they made a series of cult classic films that established them as two of the preeminent auteurs of their era: *Miller's Crossing* (1990), *Barton Fink* (1991), and *The Hudsucker Proxy* (1994) became critical darlings. But 1996's *Fargo* brought them both box office success and Academy Awards for the screenplay and Frances McDormand's acting.

No Country for Old Men marked their first film in New Mexico. The film adapted Cormac McCarthy's novel into a meditation on the changing West and the new nature of violence. In addition to some of the locations mentioned in this guide, they filmed in Albuquerque and in residential blocks of Las Vegas. The film bagged four Academy Awards, including Best Picture.

The duo returned just a few years later for another literary adaptation, this time of Charles Portis's 1968 novel *True Grit*. Although it might have seemed to be a retread of the John Wayne film of the same name, the Coens's version hewed more closely to the book. While the John Wayne version of the film was shot in Colorado, the Coens chose to use the Charles R. Ranch near Las Vegas and the San Cristobal Ranch near Santa Fe. The film also shot in Texas and Oklahoma.

Finally, the Coens revisited the Land of Enchantment in 2017 for *The Ballad of Buster Scruggs*. This Western compiled six short stories, each of which explored a traditional Western trope and often turned them upside down. In addition to filming in Diablo Canyon, the production also used Bonanza Creek Ranch, the J.W. Eaves Ranch, and the San Cristobal Ranch. Some of the more mountainous segments were shot in southern Colorado.

The Coens, though, didn't wax romantic when asked why they chose New Mexico for *No Country for Old Men*. "Oh, the rebate," said Joel Coen.

Ethan expanded a little more: "The economic incentive. As you know, the story takes place in West Texas and we shot for two weeks based in Marfa, West Texas, for the stuff you really see landscape because New Mexico offers spectacular scenery, but not of that kind and it is a very different landscape. So we shot, as everybody is in New Mexico now, for economic reasons. And because it does offer things, while it's not West Texas there are things we could shoot there we couldn't have shot in Flemington, New Jersey."

After decades of collaboration, the Coen Brothers started working on projects independently like Joel's 2021 *Tragedy of Macbeth* and Ethan's 2024 *Drive-Away Dolls*. The film was written as part of a trilogy that refocused traditional B-movies on queer heroes. The second film in the series, entitled *Honey Don't*, shot, of course, in New Mexico.

you can also reach the freeway on St. Francis Drive, or Old Pecos Trail, if you're headed to the plaza. Heading north, instead of south, I-25 connects to Eldorado, a suburb of Santa Fe, and then to Las Vegas. Eventually, the road reaches Denver. Allow six hours for that drive.

You'll find the midtown and Rufina/Siler district along Cerrillos Road. This area has benefited from a surge of interest driven by Meow Wolf (1352 Rufina Circle, Santa Fe, NM, 87507; 505-395-6369, meowwolf.com), an artist's collective, interactive exhibition, and events space. Now the area has a cooler vibe as well as new bars and restaurants.

About two blocks after you make a right turn onto Airport Road from Cerrillos Road, you'll spot an aluminum-sided warehouse that once housed Santa Fe's only indoor gun range (4230 Airport Road) and was used in *No Country for Old Men*. (An old sign for the business may still be standing, but the gun shop itself is no longer in business in this location.) In the scene, Llewelyn Moss, played by Josh Brolin, goes shopping for supplies he hopes to use to stay a step ahead of his pursuer, the vile Anton Chigurh. His conversation with a sales associate devolves into one of the many sharp, hilarious roundabouts in the film.

```
INT. SPORTING GOODS STORE—GUN COUNTER—DAY
The clerk is handing a shotgun across the counter.

                         CLERK
      Twelve gauge. You need shells?
Moss looks the gun over.

                         MOSS
      Uh-huh. Double ought.

                         CLERK
      They'll give you a wallop.
He pushes the shells across.
```

MOSS

You have camping supplies?

ANOTHER COUNTER

A clerk stares at Moss.

CLERK

Tent poles.

MOSS

Uh-huh.

CLERK

You already have the tent?

MOSS

Somethin' like that.

CLERK

Well you give me the model number of the tent. I can order you the poles.

MOSS

Never mind. I want a tent.

CLERK

What kind of tent?

MOSS

The kind with the most poles.

(From *No Country for Old Men*, adapted by Joel and Ethan Coen from the book by Cormac McCarthy)

Santa Fe's airport (121 Aviation Dr, Santa Fe, NM 87505; 505-955-2900, flysantafe.com) is on the southern end of town and offers flights to Denver, Dallas, and Phoenix. To avoid traffic on Cerrillos Road, you can take the 599 relief route to central Santa Fe.

History of Film in New Mexico

Now one of the busiest production centers in the United States, alongside New York, Atlanta, Louisiana, and Los Angeles, New Mexico boasts a long history of filmmaking that stretches back more than a century.

The Land of Enchantment featured prominently in an early "actuality," equivalent to a micro-documentary. Inventor Thomas Edison's company made a short film at Isleta Pueblo, just south of Albuquerque, only a few years after his lab created their first rudimentary motion picture devices. *Indian Day School* (1898) recorded about thirty seconds of Isleta students leaving their class room. The film was part of an Edison Company tour of the Southwest and a greater tourist campaign promoted by the railroad. (The short video is available to watch online, for those curious, at loc.gov/item/00564534/.)

Fascination with the Southwest soon brought other silent filmmakers interested in capturing the region's character. Just a decade after Edison, auteur Romaine Fielding traveled to New Mexico on his half brother's advice. A rising star at Philadelphia's Lubin Film Corporation of silent filmmakers, Fielding wanted to capture explosions at the mines near Silver City in southern New Mexico. He also wanted to document the Old West–style action then in demand among silent filmmakers. Silver City impressed Romaine so deeply that he moved all of his operations to the city.

Lubin, and other early silent film companies, preceded the Hollywood studio system and the business's preoccupation with California, where they built their palatial studios. New Mexico, in other words, wasn't simply a shooting destination in the early twentieth century, it was the company's temporary home. Fielding made himself comfortable in Silver City, and then moved his operation to Las Vegas, where the Wild West still lived on. The

Indian Day School (1898). Courtesy of the Library of Congress.

city quickly became his home for several years as he churned out reel after reel of silent films. For more on Fielding and his New Mexico operations, please see the Las Vegas driving tour on page 114.

Western star Tom Mix also set up a studio in Las Vegas. Like Fielding, Mix spent years in the rugged railroad town, cementing his reputation as one of the country's biggest Western stars. Born in Oklahoma, Mix built a career by blending genuine marksmanship and stunt skills with a larger-than-life origin story. He was, in fact, a rodeo star, who even appeared as a wrangler

Poster for Tom Mix in *The Moving Picture Cowboy* (1914).
Wikimedia Commons.

at the 1904 Louisiana Purchase Exposition in St. Louis and a bronc buster in a Wild West show. The actor also claimed to have fought in the Spanish-American War, but no evidence of his involvement exists. Tales of his war heroism, however, made his on-screen feats even more fantastic, and career embellishment was often a publicity tool for silent stars.

Mix made his first appearance for the Selig Polyscope filmmaking company in 1909, as a horse rider after the producers had spotted him at a rodeo. Thanks to his talents, Mix made a quick ascent to stardom. He churned out scores of silent films, before two officials from Las Vegas approached him and sold him on the merits of their home city. Their offer convinced Mix. He soon moved to Las Vegas and shot some two dozen films before moving on.

Fielding and Mix enjoyed fleeting fame, but neither captured a legacy like that of D. W. Griffith, who arrived in New Mexico just a few years later. Griffith would eventually be best known for directing *The Birth of a Nation* (1915). The epic silent was considered a pioneer in film technology and format, employing close-up shots, establishing shots and transitions. It also glorified the Ku Klux Klan and was outright banned in multiple cities. In New Mexico, Griffith played multiple roles—one was behind the lens of *A Pueblo Legend* (1912), and the other was on a family business venture.

Movie Set Buzzwords

In film or television production, protocol is everything. Each shooting day costs hundreds of thousands of dollars, perhaps more, and actors often have limited availability making each session urgent. Here's a few buzzwords to know, in case you run across an active film set, or if you just want to talk the talk.

Lock Up: Set production assistants will stop foot traffic to ensure that no one walks into camera frame. If people who aren't paid background talent appear on screen, a number of issues arise, including the fact that takes may not match. If you're walking around Santa Fe, you have a good chance of running into one of these.

Catering and Craft Services: Film sets are rightly famed for their chow. No matter where they set up, whether downtown or in the woods, they always bring a full spread. There are typically two places to get food on sets: catering serves the meals, three squares usually, and craft service provides snacks throughout the day.

Honeywagon or Pimo: Bathroom, typically a mobile set up much nicer than your average Porta Potty. Those headed off to the pimo can tell others they've gone "10-1" or "10-2." This is a probably a more polite euphemism than telling the unfiltered truth on the radio.

Basecamp: Set requires dozens of work trucks and a flat place to park them. The production brings most everything with them, from power to honeywagons, but any available amenities are helpful.

First Team: Usually refers to the lead cast, as opposed to their stand-ins.

Picture's Up: It's almost time to shoot.

Quiet on the Set: Which is usually when a helicopter or airplane passes by.

Roll Sound and Roll Camera: Recording is underway.

Background: The assistant directors usually give the background actors a command to get started before the leads.

Action: Yes, the first assistant director will scream this hackneyed line to get the shot started. The directors are often focused on a screen showing what the camera sees.

Cut: The action can stop.

Back to 1: After a take, the assistant director will instruct the cast to return to their starting marks.

Making the Day: Assistant directors and producers schedule every shooting day based on the location and the script. The goal is to shoot everything planned, although weather and the unpredictability of life often changes things.

Magic Hour: When the sun is coming up off the horizon or going down and the light is perfect. New Mexico and its altitude and clear skies make sunsets in the state a necessity for shows.

Wrap: End of the day or the production.

Call Sheet: A daily document that provides the film crew with an itinerary for the day's work and a report time. An accompanying map provides directions.

One-Liner: An abbreviation of the shooting schedule assembled by the assistant directors and producers. Each scene is listed by day.

Actress Mary Pickford. Library of Congress Prints and Photographs Division Washington, DC, 20540, USA. Wikimedia Commons.

Griffith's project in New Mexico, like the Edison actuality before it, made use of Isleta near Albuquerque. Instead of attempting to document the life of locals, though, the film invented a fictional and fantastical history. The silent film featured Mary Pickford as a Hopi maiden who has to come to the aid of Isleta's warriors.

At the time, Pickford was on her way to becoming one of the signature stars of the silent film era. She worked for a host of studios throughout the 1910s, until she banded together with Charlie Chaplin and Douglas Fairbanks to form United Artists and wrest control of actors' commitments back from the studios. Her star ascended even higher when she married Fairbanks, creating Hollywood's most famous—and perhaps first—power couple.

Pickford was a star but an odd choice to play a Hopi woman. Ostensibly, Griffith wanted to create an authentic representation of Native American life by hiring Isleta residents as extras and casting Pickford who supposedly had facial traits in common with Indigenous Americans. Once production began, though, it became evident that few locals would have a presence on screen.

Relations with the community deteriorated to the point that the tribe actually halted production and detained Griffith. Upset with the content of the film or the disruption that the shooting caused, the tribe was displeased with Griffith but eventually allowed him to return to work. The finished film validates the tribe's concerns. It tells the story of a shaman in search of a magical talisman, and a battle between Isleta and a group of Apaches. The story traded on stereotypes and farcical notions of Native American life. Footage still exists and is available online.

In addition to *A Pueblo Legend* and a film shot in Albuquerque called *The Tourists* (1912), Griffith was involved in a hotel financed by his brother, R. E. Griffith. Their idea was to build a hotel near the crossroads to scenic movie locations adjacent to Gallup, like Red Rocks and Monument Valley. They named their hotel El Rancho. During the golden age of filmmaking, it played host to scores of famed actors, from Clark Gable to John Wayne. El Rancho is still in business and not far from I-40 (1000 East US Route 66, Gallup, NM 87301; 505-863-9311, elranchohotelgallup.com).

The Griffiths had great foresight to anticipate that Westerns would be the dominant genre in the state. Scores of classic and not-so-classic Westerns followed in the footsteps of Tom Mix. Drawn by the state's geography and beauty, Western producers arrived in hordes to capture the Land of Enchantment on film. New Mexico's most famous resident, William H. Bonney, alias Billy the Kid, became fodder for several of these films. Director King Vidor's 1930 rendition was shot mostly in Gallup and starred football legend Johnny Mack Brown. (For more on Billy the Kid, see the sidebar on page 86.)

A number of renowned filmmakers visited the state in the following decades. Billy Wilder made the social commentary *Ace in the Hole* (1951), starring Kirk Douglas, in Gallup and Albuquerque. Douglas also starred in a similarly biting film about the changing American West called *Lonely are the Brave* (1962). Even Clint Eastwood, hot off the Spaghetti Westerns that redefined his career and the genre, got in on the act with *Hang 'Em High* (1968).

The steady demand for Western landscapes meant that two ranchers near Santa Fe could diversify their businesses by adding backlots. Eaves Ranch and Bonanza Creek Ranch both transformed from primarily cattle operations into versatile Western outdoor studios. *The Cheyenne Social Club* in 1969 was the first film to use the permanent backlot. It starred Jimmy Stewart in a comedy about an old West brothel. Meanwhile, a European Western called *Lucky Luke* (1983) got Bonanza Creek's fully built backlot started in the 1980s.

Thanks to its proximity to Los Angeles, incredible scenery, and budding infrastructure, New Mexico enjoyed a steady stream of productions until legislation opened the floodgates. Perhaps the most significant change to New Mexico's film industry arrived in 2005. Governor Gary Johnson instituted an incentive program that offered financial rewards to films and television

Tips and Resources

For the latest events and activities around town, check out one of Santa Fe's enduring weekly magazines, *The Santa Fe Reporter* (santafereporter.com) or the *Santa Fe New Mexican's* art section, *Pasatiempo* (santafenewmexican.com/pasatiempo/). Both have updated listings of arts and entertainment events. Despite the city's size and sleepy nature, there's usually something to do after the sun sets.

The State of New Mexico's Culture Pass (newmexicoculture.org/visit/culturepass) is an excellent value if you're planning on taking in several of their museums or historic sites. For $30, the pass grants admittance to the New Mexico History Museum, the Museum of Indian Arts & Culture, the Museum of International Folk Art, and the New Mexico Museum of Art. Other historic sites and museums outside of Santa Fe are included as well.

You'll need a car to see the locations listed in the back half of this book, but if you'd like to get around without one, cabs and rideshares are all available in Santa Fe. The city runs a bus system named—you guessed it—Santa Fe Trails (santafenm.gov/public-works/transit/). The Rail Runner connects to Albuquerque. More on that train in the Page to Screen tour on page 4.

shows that chose to shoot in New Mexico. Two years later, Governor Bill Richardson expanded the incentives and attracted the television projects that ultimately remade the state's image both on screen and off. In particular, *Breaking Bad* (2008), originally written to film in Southern California, relocated to Albuquerque to take advantage of the incentives.

After several seasons on air, the show entered the American zeitgeist. Not only did it redefine "Peak TV," but it also redefined the cultural map of Albuquerque. The city was maybe best known as a stop along the updated Route 66. After *Breaking Bad,* Albuquerque became synonymous with the gritty characters and drugs at the show's core.

Breaking Bad, In Plain Sight, and others also redefined New Mexico as a top-tier destination for incentivized filmmaking. A new studio south of Albuquerque with modern amenities sweetened the deal. Big-budget productions like *The Spirit* (2008), Marvel Studios' *The Avengers* (2012), and Disney's *The Lone Ranger* (2013) arrived to take advantage of these amenities. They made New Mexico one of the busiest production centers in the United States, a reputation that persists at press time.

Over the past several decades, virtually every major film studio and streaming service has shot in New Mexico. Netflix, in particular, has deep ties to the state. In 2014, the streaming giant struck a deal with the state and with the city of Albuquerque to purchase Q Studios at a discounted price tag. In exchange, Netflix promised to spend more than a billion dollars making movies and television shows locally. They also made plans to expand Q Studios to accommodate their growing slate of shows.

Governor Michelle Lujan Grisham and the New Mexico State Legislature doubled down on their investment in film by raising the cap on film spending in 2019 and again in 2023, effectively paving the way for any qualified production to take advantage of the state's aggressive rebates of 25 to 40 percent.

Get Ready for Santa Fe

Actor Timothy Blake Nelson rode toward Santa Fe with little more than his six-shooter and a fiddle in the opening minutes of the Coen Brothers' *The Ballad of Buster Scruggs* (2017). You might choose to bring a few more necessities when you arrive on your horse. Take some precautions and you'll find that your trip ends a little better than his. (Spoiler alert: the character is shot to death just minutes after his lyrical arrival.)

I'd start with clothes for infinitely variable temperatures in just about any season. Weather changes fast in Santa Fe, thanks in no small part to the elevation. Be prepared for heat and wind chills. In the summer, a hat to keep the sun off your face is an essential, as are glasses to keep the dust out of your eyes. On set, you'll often find film crew wearing Afghan scarfs called "shemaghs" to keep their necks from getting sunburned and to keep the dust off their faces. Unexpectedly, summer can bring seasonal rains usually referred to as monsoons. A rain jacket, even in the middle of the summer, is a must. In the winter, a sturdy coat and a beanie would be useful. Temperatures will dip into the teens and get much colder at elevation.

During all seasons, try to have some sunscreen and a water bottle. It's easy to get dehydrated and sunburned in New Mexico's low humidity and surprising altitude. Both minor afflictions are easily battled with a bit of precaution.

You won't have much to fear from the desert itself. Some people prefer stiffer shoes to keep cactus needles out; others prefer to walk with caution. On set, rattlesnake wranglers are hired to keep the serpents from causing a stir. In general, if you give them a wide birth, they probably won't want to expend the effort necessary to strike.

In Santa Fe, there aren't many additional dangers, aside from getting lost. You'll want the directions and maps inside this book. Use them in

Timothy Blake Nelson with Diablo Canyon in the background in
The Ballad of Buster Scruggs (2017). Courtesy of Netflix.

concert with your smartphone map for a better idea of where both film locations and activities can be found throughout Santa Fe and its environs.

If your travels take you beyond central Santa Fe, you might also consider bringing a sturdy backpack on hiking trails. Personally, I never go to set without one. On hikes, I pack first-aid supplies for any walk longer than a few miles. Most importantly, always pack water. It's often hot and dry in the high desert, and you're not likely to encounter many water fountains on your journey.

For a city its size, Santa Fe has a broad assortment of hotels in many price ranges. Several of the hotels have even served as filming locations, so look out for their occasional mention in the tours. The following selection offers some good starting points, but is far from an exhaustive list. If you're staying off the plaza, make sure to have access to a car.

Bargain Choices

The Sage Hotel (725 Cerrillos Road, Santa Fe, NM 87505; 505-982-5952, thesagesf.com). This motel is clean, close to the Railyard, and within walking distance of the plaza.

El Sendero Inn (311 Old Santa Fe Trail, Santa Fe, NM, 87501; 505-982-1851, choicehotels.com/new-mexico/santa-fe/ascend-hotels/nm268), a no-frills motel with a great location just a few feet from the plaza.

Mid-Range

Hotel Santa Fe, Hacienda & Spa (1501 Paseo de Peralta, Santa Fe, NM 87501; 855-825-9876, hotelsantafe.com), well-located between the Railyard and the plaza, this hotel has a unique distinction—it's owned, in part, by the Pueblo of Picuris.

Drury Plaza Hotel (828 Paseo de Peralta, Santa Fe, NM 87501; 505-424-2175, druryhotels.com/locations/santa-fe-nm/drury-plaza-hotel-in-santa-fe). Check out the Santa Funky tour for much more on this refurbished hospital. The Drury Plaza has become a popular choice for productions thanks to large, impeccable rooms.

Premier

Inn of the Five Graces (150 East De Vargas Street, Santa Fe, NM 87501; 505-992-0957, fivegraces.com), a posh, Middle Eastern–themed hotel right in the middle of town.

Rosewood Inn of the Anasazi (113 Washington Ave., Santa Fe, NM 87501; 505-988-3030, rosewoodhotels.com/en/inn-of-the-anasazi-santa-fe). This spacious hotel couldn't be more centrally located.

Part I

Walking Tours

The Tours

Included in this book are three unique paths through the heart of the City Different. They're arranged thematically, although if you'd prefer to find your favorite film, you can use the index or the end of each chapter to locate them. Each tour dives into the history and architecture of Santa Fe as well as into the films that made use of the city. The book isn't meant to be an exhaustive list of every film shot in the city. Instead, it's meant to introduce both Santa Fe and a select list of films and television shows worthy of your consideration. Maybe you'll decide to dial up a new movie on your favorite streaming service when you finish your walk.

Central Santa Fe is relatively flat, and the routes here are mostly on paved streets and sidewalks. If you're coming from sea level, though, don't underestimate the challenge. Even a short walk can be tough at Santa Fe's elevation. The City Different stands at 6,998 feet, more than 1,000 feet above Denver, making it the highest capital city in the United States, and the thin air is noticeable. Expect to run out of breath more quickly. You can also expect your margarita to really pack a punch.

Allow several hours for each tour, perhaps more if you plan to shop along the way. Santa Fe is widely considered one of the top destinations for art in the United States with an overall market that rivals some of the country's biggest cities. The sheer number of galleries is astounding: at least 250 of them can be found in the city's boundaries. The concentration of these galleries line historic Canyon Road, an easy walk from Santa Fe's center city. You'll find art in virtually every medium within the city, although Native American and Native American–inspired art remain the hallmark. When purchasing Indigenous work, it's always essential to check for authenticity. Fortunately, most Native artists sign their work. In some cases, the artists will be the ones selling the work themselves, leaving little doubt as to the piece's origin.

You'll also find enough food and drink to keep you fueled. Santa Fe is packed with restaurants, many of which specialize in New Mexican cuisine, which is not to be confused with its cousin from south of the border. New Mexican food is famed for its use of chiles. They're served red or green. For extra credit, you can order both at the same time, known locally as "Christmas." Recommendations for places to eat are provided throughout the tours.

TOUR 1

Page to Screen

Start: Market Street and Manhattan

Distance: 1.1 miles

Time: 50 minutes

Highlights: The Santa Fe Railyard, Bataan Memorial Building, Evangelo's Cocktail Lounge, the Palace of the Governors

Parking: Metered street parking is available throughout the area.

Not ready to walk yet? Maybe you can catch a ride on a chariot or a magical beast. Santa Fe is home to both, at least on the printed page. You can meet your flying serpent in the Railyard, a trendy, growing section of town, where there's plenty to do and even more to drink. (You'll notice a painting of a dragon on the back of the Jean Cocteau Cinema, but more on this spectacle soon.)

The Atchison, Topeka and Santa Fe Railway first reached Santa Fe in 1880, connecting Santa Fe through a rail spur in the Galisteo Basin at present-day Lamy. The depot and the area around it filled with tourists, travelers, and activities. The Santa Fe Depot remained busy for decades but was dilapidated by the end of twentieth century. The city declared it "blighted" in 1987, and marked the district for redevelopment, The city began to rehabilitate the Railyard in 2004.*

Some of the buildings in the Railyard date back a century including the stucco-fronted depot you'll see to the left of the tracks. The depot was constructed in 1880 and recently received a facelift. It still serves as the station for the New Mexico Rail Runner (1-866-795-RAIL, riometro.org), a commuter train that travels from Belen to Albuquerque to Santa Fe. The

* https://sfrailyardcc.org/the-railyard/history/

Rail Runner makes for a pleasant alternative route to Santa Fe, even though trains run infrequently during non-commuter hours.

As part of its revitalization, the Railyard added a multiplex theater called the Sky Cinemas (formerly Violet Crown Cinema) at (1606 Alcaldesa Street, Santa Fe, NM 87501; 505-216-5678, santafe.violetcrown.com), an REI (500 Market Street Suite 100, Santa Fe, NM 87501; 505-982-3557, rei.com/stores/santa-fe) and Sky Coffee (1609a Alcaldesa Street, Santa Fe, NM 87501; skysantafe.com).

More than a few bars and breweries have since popped up, including Second Street Brewery (1607 Paseo de Peralta, Santa Fe NM 87501; 505-989-3278, secondstreetbrewery.com/railyard) and Nuckolls (1611 Alcaldesa Street, Santa Fe, NM 87501; nuckollsbrewing.com). Across the tracks, there's a distillery for the harder stuff called As Above So Below (545 Camino de la Familia, Santa Fe, NM 87501; aasbdistillery.com). For those

The Santa Fe Railyard. Photograph by Rennett Stowe, Wikimedia Commons.

really interested in sampling additional beverages try Santa Fe Spirits (308 Read Street, Santa Fe, NM 87501; 505-780-5906, santafespirits.com), just up Read Street from the Railyard.

On Saturdays, the Santa Fe Farmers' Market (1607 Paseo de Peralta, Santa Fe, NM 87501; 505-983-4098, santafefarmersmarket.com), held at the southern end of the tracks, brings in fresh food from all over the region.

Grab a coffee (if you're anything like the author of this book, walking tours often transform into coffee tastings; several recommendations can be found throughout this guide), and then head to the Jean Cocteau Cinema (418 Montezuma Avenue, Santa Fe, NM, 87501; 505-466-5528, jeancocteaucinema.com) at the end of the railroad tracks, taking note of the two separate trains you'll pass along the way. Stop when you reach the end of the tracks and enjoy the view of both the theater and the trains.

Named for French playwright, novelist, and filmmaker Jean Cocteau, the cinema first opened in 1976, as the Collective Fantasy theater. Seven years later, it was renamed the Cocteau and stayed open for another two decades until multiplex theaters elsewhere in Santa Fe put it out of business in 2006. (The Violet Crown, also in the Railyard, was not built until 2015.) Then, American novelist, screenwriter, television producer, and short story writer George R. R. Martin rescued the inauspicious venue.

Famed for writing the fantasy series *A Song of Ice and Fire,* usually called *A Game of Thrones,* Martin moved to Santa Fe in 1979 and often contemplated owning a theater that would screen camp and cult classics at midnight. One day, Martin drove past the vacant Cocteau, and it occurred to him that he could afford to make his dream a reality. He reopened the Cocteau as The Jean Cocteau Cinema in 2013, and devoted it to independent film, live shows, and, of course, book signings. The theater also received a liquor license and regularly serves cocktails inspired by their screenings or Martin's characters, including The Night's Watch, A Slice of Heaven, and, of course, the George R. R. Martini.

In addition to salvaging the Cocteau, Martin also invested in restoring the scenic Southern Santa Fe Railway. Now known as the Sky Railway (430

West Manhattan Avenue, Santa Fe, NM 87501; 844-743-3759, skyrailway.com), the short spur line travels about eleven miles to the junction at Lamy, New Mexico. When originally completed in the late nineteenth century, the short line connected Santa Fe to the Denver & Rio Grande, dubbed the Chili Line, making the small territorial capitol accessible without long and painful rides on buckboard wagons. The spur has operated intermittently as a tourist line, and Martin and a management group that includes author Douglas Preston took ownership of it in 2020 to revamp it as a luxurious rail experience complete with beer tastings, burlesque shows, stargazing events, sunsets, historical lectures, murder mysteries, and jazz.

If you take the train, you'll reach an additional filming location at the southern terminus. The Lamy train station is home to the Legal Tender Saloon & Eating House (151 Old Lamy Trail, Santa Fe, NM 87504; 505-466-1650, legaltenderlamy.com). Built in 1881 as a general store, the building became a saloon before World War II and eventually, the Legal Tender in 1969. The Victorian Era–charm, and its location at the end of the tracks, have made the saloon and restaurant a local favorite. The restaurant was recently revamped by the ownership group behind Las Vegas' Castañeda. You can spot the bar in the fourth episode of the first season of *Outer Range* (2022), starring Josh Brolin and Imogen Poots. The series might best be described as a Western crossed with sci-fi. As of this writing, the show has dropped two seasons on Amazon Prime Video. *Outer Range* otherwise made use of private properties around Santa Fe.

Amazingly, the show wasn't the first to blend these genres and film in Santa Fe. The attempted blockbuster *Cowboys & Aliens* (2011) smashed together an extraterrestrial film with a spaghetti-style Western. The film had all the ingredients for success, including hitmaker Jon Favreau behind the camera, stars Harrison Ford and Daniel Craig, and the writers-producers of the *Star Trek* franchise reboot. Audiences responded to the hype, but weren't sure what to do about the film itself. Director Jon Favreau reportedly had to tell crowds that the movie wasn't a comedy, but more serious action-adventure fare. Unfortunately, the joke turned out to be on

On the train in *Oppenheimer* (2023). Courtesy of Universal Pictures.

the studio as the film radically underperformed at the box office. *Cowboys & Aliens* was shot largely at Bonanza Creek Ranch.

Beyond science fiction, the train to Lamy played a major part in the scientific past. In its original incarnation, the spur line carried personnel for the Manhattan Project during World War II. Some eighty years later, filmmaker Christopher Nolan's historical drama *Oppenheimer* (2023) took advantage of the railway. Based on the 2005 book *American Prometheus: The Triumph and Tragedy of J. Robert Oppenheimer* by Kai Bird, Nolan's super-secretive film shot in Santa Fe as well as in Los Alamos.

To recreate the journey to Santa Fe along the same path once used by the real people, Nolan's team commandeered the tourist railway. In the scenes they filmed, Cillian Murphy's J. Robert Oppenheimer trades barbs with Matt Damon's Leslie Groves about the burden of their top-secret project. To make it period-accurate, production partially restored two Pullman cars with dining and sleeping sections. The rest of the crew rode behind in the flatbed car or in one of the cars emblazoned with a painting of a dragon.

The Sky Railway isn't the only antique train in the state. Perhaps the most famous railroad in New Mexico is located several hours northwest of Santa Fe in Chama, New Mexico. The Cumbres & Toltec Scenic Railroad is the remnant of a late-nineteenth-century route to silver mines in Durango, Colorado. The narrow-gauge railroad fell out of use but was restored by a local committee. The train, and the majestic mountains through which it winds, are on display in a number of Westerns like *The Good Guys and the Bad Guys* (1969), *Bite the Bullet* (1975), *Wyatt Earp* (1994), *The Legend of the Lone Ranger* (1981), and *Butch & Sundance: The Early Days* (1979).

As you look at the pair of railroad tracks at the Railyard, the more modern line, closest to the station, is the commuter Rail Runner, mentioned above. The Sky Railway is often stationed just to the left as you face the end of the tracks. Please use caution if you want a closer look at the locomotives as both trains are still active.

Go past the end of the tracks and the theater to the attached Beastly Books. For those looking for a souvenir from New Mexico television royalty, this is a great spot. The boutique store specializes in sci-fi and fantasy literature. Here, you'll find volumes signed by Martin and other authors (418 Montezuma Avenue, Santa Fe, New Mexico 87501; 505-395-2628, beastlybooks.com). As you exit the Cocteau Cinema or Beastly Books, turn to the left and go about half a block to New Mexico School for the Arts.

Now a charter school, this building was once a mall called the SanBusCo Market Center. The structure itself began life as the Santa Fe Builders Supply Company in 1880, providing lumber that could be transported via rail. For years, the mall's parking lot was wedged into the old lumber shelves behind the main building.

If you turn right as you exit Jean Cocteau Cinema or Beastly Books, you'll see the Vladem Contemporary (404 Montezuma Avenue, Santa Fe, NM 87501; 505-476-5063, nmartmuseum.org/vladem-contemporary), the southern wing of the New Mexico Museum of Art and a recent addition to Santa Fe's sprawling collection of art institutions. It opened in late 2023. The museum is built in a remodeled 1930s warehouse that once served as the state archives. From the Vladem, head up Montezuma past Guadalupe and Sandoval streets to Galisteo Street. You can cross Galisteo to the courtyard directly ahead.

On your right, the Bataan Memorial Building began life as the New Mexico Territorial Capital in 1900. Originally built in the neoclassical style of architecture, characterized by a grandeur of scale and a dramatic use of columns, the building was completely overhauled in 1951 to make it look more New Mexican in the Territorial Revival style, often characterized by simple textures, such as brick or adobe, and Greek- or Gothic-style trimmings. The colonnades and the dome were both removed, although you can spot the old cupola through the glass in the central tower.

The Bataan Memorial Building. Photograph by GiantRobot, Wikimedia Commons.

In 1966, when the Roundhouse opened, the old state capitol was repurposed as governmental offices and renamed the Bataan Memorial Building in tribute to military service members who died on the Bataan Death March, a World War II catastrophe that claimed the lives of many New Mexican soldiers. These men had previously been part of the National Guard before they were assigned to regiments in the Philippines, where they were captured and forcibly marched to prisoner of war camps. Outside the building, an eternal flame burns in remembrance of the fallen. A nearby marker, taken from the Guardsmen's post in Texas, is emblazoned with the state's Zia Sun emblem.

Historical writer, journalist, and Santa Fe resident Hampton Sides detailed the experience of the Bataan Death March in his best-selling 2001 book *Ghost Soldiers: The Forgotten Epic Account of World War II's Most Dramatic Mission*. The book was eventually adapted into a film called the *Great Raid* (2005). The film starred James Franco as an imprisoned American soldier trying to survive the atrocities of a Japanese prison camp. While Sides conducted much of his research in and around Santa Fe, the film was shot elsewhere.

You can also spot the Bataan Memorial Building in both *Waco* (2018) and *Waco: The Aftermath* (2023). The first season focused on the siege of the Branch Davidian compound in Waco, Texas, in 1993. Taylor Kitsch, best known for his role in the televised version of *Friday Night Lights*, starred in a career-redefining role. Other featured actors included Michael Shannon, Julia Garner, Rory Culkin, and John Leguizamo. Almost all of the series unfolded in a recreated version of the historical group's compound, built near Galisteo. In the third episode of *Waco* season 1, Michael Shannon, playing expert FBI negotiator Gary Noesner, exits his office after using the gym and having an argument with his superiors at work. The rear of the Bataan Memorial Building is clearly visible in this scene. The second season of the show staged a press conference in the building.

Oppenheimer transformed the building into an approximation of Washington, DC, to recreate the 1959 confirmation hearing of Atomic

Energy Commission Chairman Lewis Strauss. The production turned a grand hearing room into a mid-century space. They also found spots in the Bataan Memorial Building for a committee hearing room and Senate offices. Robert Downey Jr., who once played Iron Man for Marvel in *The Avengers*, which shot in Albuquerque, gained critical acclaim for his portrayal of Strauss, doing much of his heavy lifting in this building.

The Bataan Memorial Building is open to the public, although it houses a number of executive branch offices like the New Mexico Department of Veteran Services. A small exhibit featuring mementos from the careers of service members pays additional homage to the military personnel of New Mexico. Check out the exterior of the building, have a peek inside, and then exit the building the way you initially arrived and make a right on Galisteo Street toward the Santa Fe Plaza. Cross over the Santa Fe River, which used to flow year-round and is now a seasonal stream, and go two blocks to Collected Works bookstore (202 Galisteo Street, Santa Fe, NM 87501; 505-988-4226, collectedworksbookstore.com).

One of Santa Fe's oldest bookstores, Collected Works has a regular series of speakers and community book discussions. For additional book shopping, try Op.Cit. Books (157 Paseo de Peralta, Santa Fe, NM 87501; 505-428-0321, opcit.com), or Garcia Street Books (376 Garcia Street, Santa Fe, NM 87501; 505-986-0151, garciastreetbooks.com). After buying multiple copies of books by the author of this tour, exit the bookstore. You can also fulfill your New Mexico reading list at Collected Works. Check out the sidebar Santa Fe in Books on page 15 for some suggestions on other local books worth reading and literary doings.

Head straight up Galisteo Street one block to Evangelo's Cocktail Lounge (200 West San Francisco Street, Santa Fe, NM 87501; evangeloscocktaillounge.com). The bar has hosted two literary adaptations, both featuring Jeff Bridges. The Scott Cooper–directed film *Crazy Heart* was based on the Thomas Cobb novel of the same name, while the firefighter drama *Only the Brave* (2017) was inspired by a magazine article written by Sean Flynn and published in 2013 in *GQ* called "No Exit."

Jeff Bridges as Bad Blake in Evangelo's from *Crazy Heart* (2009). Courtesy of Fox Searchlight Pictures.

Evangelo's makes a natural setting for a raucous bar and concert hall, because that's exactly what it is in real life. Named for a Greek immigrant and World War II veteran, once the subject of a famed war photographer Eugene Smith, the bar has regularly hosted live music since the 1970s. At press time, the bar hosts at least two concerts per week. Check out their website for listings.

Likewise, it's no stretch of the imagination to put Jeff Bridges on screen as a singer. Bridges began his career as a musician in 2000, a full five decades after he started acting. Since then, he's released one solo album and one with his band, Jeff Bridges and the Abiders. That band, of course, is named for his most famous quote in the Coen Bros' classic *The Big Lebowski* (1998): "The dude abides." Bridges also recorded tracks for the *Crazy Heart* album, released alongside the film.

On screen, Bridges plays Otis "Bad" Blake, a middle-aged, former country-and-western star whose life and career are both on the skids. He drinks to excess, schedules performances at lowly bowling alleys, and is completely alienated from his family, in part because he's always on the road. He can't even afford to re-up on his favorite whiskey and relies on the kindness of a fan to get his next fix.

Through the drink and the depression, Blake keeps performing. In addition to his bowling alley gig, he's also booked a small, live music bar in Santa Fe (Evangelo's) where he meets an aspiring journalist played by Maggie Gyllenhaal, with whom he quickly falls in love. Blake sees his new romance as a chance to redeem himself in life and in family.

His alcoholism, though, diverts his plans and soon, Blake loses his new family. His troubles inspire him to write a new song, which he titles "The Weary Kind." The song brings Blake deserved accolades and a new lease on his musical career. Blake reunites with his former mentee, the superstar performer Tommy Sweet (played by Colin Farrell in a surprising cameo), who quickly turns the songs Blake writes into hits.

Off-screen, the song was also a major hit. Cowritten by famed producer T Bone Burnett and New Mexico native Ryan Bingham, the song netted an Academy Award. Bingham played a small role in the film as a band member at the bowling alley and then returned to work with director Scott Cooper on the Western *Hostiles* (2017). When not making cameos on film, Bingham has spent time all over the Southwest and recorded five albums, including 2010s *Junky Star*.

After *Crazy Heart*, Bridges came back to Evangelo's to perform on the bar's stage once again for a scene in *Only the Brave*. Playing fire chief Duane Steinbrink, Bridges highlights a party for the Granite Mountain Hotshots. The scene is based on a real-life party in which Steinbrink and his band, The Rusty Pistols, performed for a group of Hot Shot firefighters. Amazingly, the real-life band members played themselves in the scene. Bridges even convinced producer T Bone Burnett to arrange the song for the scene—a cover of Stan Jones's classic country-and-western jingle "Ghost Riders in the Sky."

Most of the elite firefighters depicted in the scene, however, ultimately perished in the 2013 Yarnell Hill Fire, an 8,000-acre burn that spread due to high winds south of Prescott, Arizona. Nineteen Granite Mountain Hotshots

Santa Fe in Books

The capital of Southwestern art attracts more than paintbrushes—it also attracts pens. Or, at least, those who wield them. In addition to the authors mentioned throughout this book like Willa Cather, George R. R. Martin, Douglas Preston, Lew Wallace, Richard Bradford, Hampton Sides, Cormac McCarthy, and John Nichols, Santa Fe was also home to the likes of Paul Horgan, Charlie Siringo, and David Morrell.

Pulitzer Prize winner Horgan wrote extensively about the Southwest in both fiction and nonfiction. Perhaps his best-known work is *Great River: The Rio Grande in American History*, published in 1955, which netted a Pulitzer and Bancroft Prize. He was also lauded for a biography of Archbishop Lamy, released in 1975. Willa Cather also wrote about Lamy. You can find more on him and the cathedral associated with his legacy in the Santa Funky tour on page 56.

Siringo is frequently associated with the popularization of cowboy lore. A former lawman, ranch hand, and detective, he memorialized his experiences in the book *A Texas Cowboy; or, Fifteen Years on the Hurricane Deck of a Spanish Pony* in 1885, which became a national bestseller. Even so, Siringo continued his work as a detective for the Pinkertons, eventually retiring to Santa Fe in 1907. There, he wrote additional books including a biography of his supposed acquaintance, Billy the Kid.

Siringo also dabbled with the film industry. After struggling with his physical and financial health, he moved from Santa Fe to Los Angeles, where he consulted on films and took small roles in Westerns. He even tried his hand at screenwriting. Siringo's Hollywood adventures, though, never lived up to his literary escapades.

You can drive down Siringo Road, but that's the closest you'll get to Charlie himself. If you'd like to meet some writers in person, the best bet would be the Santa Fe International Literary Festival, which kicked off in 2022, putting Santa Fe's reputation as a book hub to good use. The annual event is held at the Convention Center and features a gallery of established writers from around the world like Amy Tan, Terry Tempest Williams and David Grann (sfinternationallitfest.org). The spring event might be worth circling on your calendar if you're interested in adding signed books to your Santa Fe bounty. You can also keep an eye on Op. Cit. Books, Collected Works, or Garcia Street Books for more literary happenings.

Bailey Chase as Branch Connally goes in search of his assailant deep in the bowels of the Matador in the third season of *Longmire* (2012–2017). Courtesy of Netflix.

lost their lives in the blaze. The party and Bridges's onstage act made for a final moment of levity before tragedy befell them in this fictionalized retelling of events.

For a different drinking vibe, or perhaps additional drinks, try the Matador Bar across San Francisco Street from Evangelo's. This subterranean nightclub is popular with Santa Fe's younger crowd. The Matador is a no-frills establishment that sells canned and bottled beers for cash only. It's a natural destination for an off-the-book investigation that includes more than a few drinks, which is exactly what the square-jawed lawman Branch Connally does in the third season of the cowboy procedural show, *Longmire* (2012–2017).

Played by Bailey Chase, Connally, a deputy in the sheriff's office of fictional Absaroka County in Wyoming, searches the Denver underworld for a ghostly hitman. As his investigation unfolds, Connally slowly loses his mind. He makes a stark contrast to his boss, the hard-edged, straight-shooting, titular Sheriff Walt Longmire. Although Longmire and Connally have something of a running feud, there is little Longmire could do to stop Connally's descent into darkness.

The *Longmire* show was based on a series of novels by Craig Johnson. Originally from West Virginia, Johnson moved to Wyoming, where he built his dream ranch by hand. During construction, he began writing a novel about a sheriff named Walter Longmire. Johnson told *The New York Times* that he put the manuscript in a drawer, only to pick it up years later and finish it after much deliberation. To date, he's written nineteen books in the series. The books and show focus on the Absaroka County sheriff's department in a crime-addled section of Wyoming on the border with the Cheyenne Reservation.

Johnson's hero Sheriff Longmire relies on the "code of the West" and on the wisdom of his Native American advisor and friend Henry Standingbear, played by Lou Diamond Phillips, to keep the peace. Australian Robert Taylor donned his best American accent for the part. He described his character to *Collider*: "He's decent, he's restrained, he's old school, he's not demonstrative. He's the kind of man I like. It's what you do when no one is watching you, how honest you are and how you carry yourself. In a modern world, he's got one foot in both camps and he's torn."

Something of a hit for A&E, the network still decided to drop the show after three seasons because the viewership skewed older, making the show less valuable to potential advertisers. After news of the cancellation spread, a dedicated group of fans rallied online to find a new home for the show. Netflix came to the rescue, ultimately funding the show for three additional seasons.

The show shot mostly around Las Vegas and Santa Fe. For details on the Las Vegas sites, check out the driving tour on page 114. Several Santa Fe locations are sprinkled throughout the walking tours. Perhaps the show's most iconic spot was Longmire's cabin, shot at Valles Caldera National Preserve. You can find details on Longmire's cabin in the North of Santa Fe and Outdoor Adventure driving tour (page 97).

The chariot race from *Ben-Hur* (1924). Wikimedia Commons. Courtesy of MGM/UA.

Finish your beer before heading out of the Matador and making a right up West San Francisco Street toward the Santa Fe Plaza and across it, toward the Palace of the Governors. (You can find more on the plaza itself in the Santa Fe Trail chapter on page 41.) A classic film came of age in this historic adobe building, even though it never shot a day in New Mexico.

In a room just off the plaza, Territorial Governor Lew Wallace wrote the closing chapters of his long-gestating opus about a betrayed Jewish prince and his search for belief. Wallace actually began the novel years earlier but finished it in Santa Fe where he had been assigned by President Rutherford B. Hayes to quell the violence in southern New Mexico, known nationally as the Lincoln County War. Wallace managed to finish the book, which he called *Ben Hur: A Tale of the Christ* (1881).

The book spawned stage plays and multiple films, most notably William Wyler's 1959 version that starred Charlton Heston. *Ben Hur* received the most Academy Awards of any feature film until James Cameron's *Titanic* surpassed it in 1998.

The Palace of the Governors is a classic in its own right. Initially built between 1610 and 1612 for use as the capital of New Mexico in the Kingdom of New Spain, the adobe structure had as many as eighteen rooms in its original form. Early incarnations of the palace also had defensive features including parapets and several *torreones*, or towers.

Despite these castle-like additions, the palace was overrun during the Pueblo Revolt in 1680, when Pueblo peoples, in search of religious and personal freedom, overthrew the Spanish colonists and retook possession of New Mexico. In the process, much of the Palace of the Governors was destroyed. The Spanish retook Santa Fe in 1692, and began to renovate the Palace of the Governors, completing the restoration by the 1730s.

Although still in use as the seat of government, the palace was aged and in disrepair when the Wallaces arrived on 1878. Susan Wallace discovered a collection of rotting records that she insisted be preserved. They became the center of the Spanish Archives of New Mexico. The Wallaces themselves stayed in New Mexico Territory only three years. Lew Wallace moved back East when his novel became a bestseller. Susan also wrote a book while in New Mexico titled *Land of the Pueblos* (1888); Susan had less than kind

Architecture Primer

While Santa Fe counts among the oldest of North American cities, about the same age as Quebec in Canada, Jamestown in Virginia, and St. Augustine in Florida, its antique veneer is actually just that—a veneer. Much of the city was intentionally rebuilt to integrate its signature Pueblo Revival and Territorial styles. The aesthetics reflected centuries of cultural and hegemonic change.

The greatest influence on the city's look may be the earliest. The Pueblo style of adobe construction, using natural bricks or packed mud, was adopted from ancient Native American traditions of construction in the Southwest. Spanish colonists added to the technique by molding bricks and adding a clay and straw matrix. Once the adobe walls were built, they were topped with low roofs built upon vigas and latillas, which became a hallmark of the city's (and state's) architecture. The Pueblos had also introduced smaller, efficient doorways. Exposed vigas, most of which are nonfunctional endcaps, and these compact-style doors are unmistakable around town.

In addition to their adobe technique, the Spanish brought

a clay finish to their walls, giving the adobe a more polished look. To get between these comfortable rooms, the colonists brought the portals popular in Mexico. These simple passageways often also included rough vigas and latillas.

The American period resulted in additional changes to the town's style. Americans popularized pitched roofs, and, eventually, red bricks among the buildings—a telltale sign of Territorial styling and easy to spot on your walks. They also introduced Victorian elements like gables and iron railings. Perhaps most importantly, the new wave of residents wanted to update the city to their tastes. Traditional adobe buildings gave way to structures that leaned heavily on European influences. As Santa Fe grew with the railroad, it shunted aside its past.

The past, though, was not to be ignored much longer. A surge of interest in Southwestern archaeology, coupled with the restoration of the Palace of the Governors, began a movement toward returning the city to its stylistic roots. Santa Fe's most distinctive aesthetic, Pueblo Revival, emerged in the greater Southwest in the early 1900s and included influences drawn from the Spanish Colonial, Mission, and the Pueblos of New Mexico. Design highlights usually include the exposed vigas that emerge near the top of the flat roofs and stucco or adobe walls. The style truly blossomed when New Mexico became a state in 1912 and its capital city adopted the look to mark itself as a uniquely Southwestern city. Greater Santa Fe Style now usually refers to Pueblo Revival, Territorial, and Spanish Mission aesthetics, all of which you will see during these tours.

The movement toward a beautiful, unique Santa Fe became law in the 1950s when a zoning law mandated that buildings in the central Santa Fe historic district adhere to traditional Santa Fe style including low profiles, flat roofs, and stucco. The City Different's charm, in other words, is enshrined by law.

General Lew Wallace in his study, 1901. Wikimedia Commons.

The Palace of the Governors, from Annual Report of the Secretary of the Interior, June 30, 1897. Wikimedia Commons.

things to say about her temporary home, exclaiming that the United States should return the territory to Old Mexico.

The palace itself turned into a historical keepsake not long after the Wallaces departed. A new capitol building was finished in 1889, and the palace became the property of the Museum of New Mexico and was then remodeled between 1909 and 1912. The palace's porch, previously a blend of Colonial and Greek Revival styles, was renovated to fit Santa Fe's emerging aesthetic. Using designs preserved from 1776, the Museum of New Mexico rehabilitated the porch to look more Spanish Colonial and regional revival in nature.

Today, that same porch is part of an arts program for Native American craftspeople to sell their wares. To qualify, artists have to apply and show proof of their Indigenous ancestry. The result is a unique opportunity to purchase Native American art, including pottery and silver jewelry, directly from Native artists.

The Palace of the Governors itself is part of the New Mexico History Museum, which opened in 2009. It includes exhibits on the ancient and recent history of the state as well as a library. Inside the Palace of the Governors, you'll find the Ben Hur room, where Wallace finished his novel. The Press at the Palace of the Governors, known informally as the Palace Press and located on the north side of the museum courtyard, is the oldest traditional printer in the state and hosts printing and bookmaking workshops, introducing visitors to the world of nineteenth- and early-twentieth-century publishing and printmaking.

The filmed adaptation of Richard Bradford's 1968 coming-of-age novel *Red Sky at Morning* shot briefly near the portico of the palace. A rose-colored portrayal of a lightly fictionalized version of Santa Fe, called Corazon Sagrado, the book follows a military family that relocates to Santa Fe from Mobile, Alabama. The move is a shock for teenager Josh Arnold, who quickly learns about the area's diverse population and runs into trouble with the local bully, although it's the bully himself who ultimately becomes the victim of violence.

The story resounds with sincerity because the book's author first visited Santa Fe as a child and then made it his full-time home as an adult. Although born in Chicago and educated in New Orleans, Bradford developed a keen understanding of New Mexico's essential characters. He wrote copy for the State of New Mexico tourism office for much of his career and then authored one more book set in the area before retiring as a novelist and living the rest of his life in the state. His familiarity with the region comes to life in one of the more memorable scenes both in the film and the book: Bradford's protagonist receives an introductory lecture on the proper racial etiquette and terminology used in the area. The speech is insightful, if not accurate.

In another pivotal sequence, before Arnold and the sheriff mount up their search for the wayward bad guy, they meet up quickly at the plaza, with the Palace of the Governors in the background. The final showdown takes place outside of the Santa Fe city limits, where the bad guy has holed up. A foot-chase sequence shot near the corner of Camino Don Miguel and Acequia Madre is an easy walk from Canyon Road and an optional extension to the Santa Funky tour. For now, make sure to explore the interior of the New Mexico History Museum.

Then cross over the park to La Fonda on the Plaza (100 E. San Francisco Street, Santa Fe, NM 87501; 505-982-5511, lafondasantafe.com), where *Ride the Pink Horse* (1947) was filmed. The film follows an army veteran who travels to the fictional town of San Pablo, New Mexico, where he hopes to hoodwink a local gangster into a payment. Robert Montgomery directed the film and starred as un-enlightened antihero Lucky Gagin who proves better at tossing tired stereotypes at locals than he is at actually shaking down the film's villain for a purse.

Part of Gagin's trouble is that he has arrived at a busy time when the streets are packed. Much like Santa Fe, San Pablo holds an annual celebration of the Spanish Reconquest. The real-life Fiestas de Santa Fe are held every

The plaza as it appears in *Red Sky at Morning* (1971). Courtesy of Universal Pictures.

Labor Day weekend and similarly fete the return of Spanish rule in 1692. The weekend-long event includes processions, mariachi performances, melodramas and, most famously, the Burning of Zozobra, or Old Man Gloom (burnzozobra.com).

Santa Feans have gathered en masse to watch a fifty-foot marionette burn for a century. Artist William Howard "Will" Shuster Jr. created the tradition in 1924, drawing inspiration from Easter Holy Week traditions among the Yaquis of the state of Sonora in northwestern Mexico. The first marionettes in Santa Fe were much smaller but have grown to their present size over time. The now fifty-foot effigy is typically filled with thousands of notes detailing people's woes, regrets, and bad memories from the past year. Made of steel wire on a wooden frame and covered with cotton cloth, Zozobra sways and waves as he is engulfed in flames. It takes thousands of people to build the marionette and a small team to manipulate him during the event. A fictionalized Zozobra-like figure makes an appearance in *Ride the Pink Horse* as Gagin navigates the town.

San Pablo's close resemblance to Santa Fe can be traced to the personal experiences of author Dorothy B. Hughes, who wrote the novel but didn't adapt it herself. Hughes was born in 1904 in Missouri and went on to a career as a writer and fiction reviewer. All told, she wrote fourteen novels, many of which draw comparisons to the works of Dashiell Hammett. The novels, and the films they inspired, are mostly noir. The bulk of her books were published around World War II and deal with the aftermath of the war in the diversifying American West. Three of Hughes's books have been adapted into film, including *In a Lonely Place* (1950), which starred Humphrey Bogart as Dix Steele, a World War II veteran with violent tendencies; *The Fallen Sparrow*, which was released in 1943; and *Ride the Pink Horse*, which was actually adapted to screen twice: in Montgomery's film and in a made-for-TV-movie by the same name released in 1962—the first film shot in the hallways of the La Fonda hotel.

Another noir, *White Sands* (1992), also gives the La Fonda a starring role. The film features Willem Dafoe as a small-town cop who steps into the shoes of a slain bagman in order to find a murderer. The search takes him to La Fonda, where he rendezvous with a schlocky Mickey Rourke and a social activist played by Mary Elizabeth Mastrantonio. Dafoe finds himself getting uncomfortably deep in his assumed role, with the journey getting more and more dangerous as the film goes on.

Produced by James G. Robinson, the film rolls out a murderer's row of 1990s character actors like Miguel Sandoval, James Rebhorn, Maura Tierney, and M. Emmet Walsh. Look for Samuel L. Jackson, on the cusp of stardom, playing a less-than-sympathetic FBI agent. The film shot all over New Mexico including, of course, the White Sands National Park where the story comes to a bloody end.

Although *White Sands* shares a location with *Ride the Pink Horse* and a history of noir filmmaking, the film's writer, Daniel Pyne, points to other inspirations like Alfred Hitchcock's *North by Northwest* (1959) and Orson

Welles's *Touch of Evil* (1958). A child of the Southwest, Pyne also looked at Westerns like *Treasure of the Sierra Madre* (1948) and Walter Hill's *Extreme Prejudice* (1987). Pyne even drew inspiration from the writings of Tony Hillerman. (More on that mystery writer later.)

You can explore the lobby of La Fonda and even eat in the hotel's central restaurant, La Plazuela. Stick around after you've finished your meal, the next tour starts right here.

La Fonda Hotel at the end of the Santa Fe Trail, Boston Public Library, Print Department, 1922. Wikimedia Commons.

Selected Filmography

Cooper, Scott, dir. *Crazy Heart*. Fox Searchlight Pictures, 2009. Film.

Baldwin, Hunt, and John Coveny, creators. *Longmire*. A+E Networks, 2012–2017. TV series.

Donaldson, Roger, dir. *White Sands*. Warner Bros., 1992. Film.

Dowdle, John Eric and Drew, creators. *Waco*. Paramount Network, 2018. TV series.

Dowdle, John Eric and Drew, creators. *Waco: The Aftermath*. Showtime Network, 2023. TV series.

Goldstone, James, dir. *Red Sky at Morning*. Universal Pictures, 1971. Film.

Montgomery, Robert, dir. *Ride the Pink Horse*. Universal Pictures, 1947. Film.

Kosinski, Joseph, dir. *Only the Brave*. Columbia Pictures, 2017. Film.

Nolan, Christopher, dir. *Oppenheimer*. Universal Pictures, 2023. Film.

Watkins, Brian, creator. *Outer Range*. Amazon Studios, 2022. TV series.

TOUR 2

Spooky and Spectacular Santa Fe

Start: Loretto Chapel: 207 Old Santa Fe Trail

Distance: 1.2 miles

Time: 45 minutes

Highlights: La Fonda on the Plaza, Plaza Café, 109 East Palace Avenue, La Posada, Loretto Chapel

Parking: Parking can be difficult around the plaza, so leave time to find a metered spot. Alternatively, try the paid lot at 121 Sandoval Street.

Santa Fe has had four hundred years to collect both phantasms and the fantastic. Ghost stories abound in the City Different, but a few of the most popular haunts are fit for the living, the dead, and the filmed. If you've stayed at La Plazuela (100 E. San Francisco St. Santa Fe NM 87501; 505-982-5511, lafondasantafe.com/la-plazuela) to eat after the previous tour, you may have already seen a few of them.

Reportedly, the ghosts of a hanged gambler and that of murdered Territorial Supreme Court Justice John P. Slough are often seen in the restaurant. Other phantasms have been sighted throughout the hotel, often spotted so frequently that the hotel staff regard these sightings as routine.

It's not surprising that the hotel has guests from another century—the building is quite old. In its current form, La Fonda celebrated its centennial in 2022, but the first inn on the spot operated as early as 1607. In 1851, a one-story building called the Exchange Hotel was built around a central courtyard. Then, in 1919, La Fonda was reconstructed to incorporate a more regional look.

The new La Fonda had Pueblo Revival touches throughout, including a courtyard entrance and forty-six guest rooms on the upper floor. Inside were many of the hallmarks of modern Santa Fe style like exposed vigas, wooden beams on the ceilings, local tin work, and Navajo rugs. The Fred Harvey Company acquired the hotel in 1926, and famed architects John Gaw Meem and Mary Colter made the hotel even more distinctly Southwestern.

Titans of the late-nineteenth and early-twentieth-century travel industry, the Harvey Company ran hotels and restaurants with buttoned-up service along the Atchison, Topeka and Santa Fe rail line. To promote their accommodations, they branded, packaged, and sold the Southwest, essentially inventing Southwestern tourism in the process, including their "Indian Detours" program, which offered automobile trips to New Mexico Pueblos.

The company, especially its employees, were immortalized in a 1946 film called *The Harvey Girls,* starring Judy Garland and Angela Lansbury as titular Harvey Girls. The prim and proper Harvey Girls head west as the keepers of society in the order-less frontier, and Garland and Lansbury find their way into their midst when plans at marriage go awry. The film, though, was shot mostly in California.

La Fonda pops up in a number of features and television shows. Look for it in *Perpetual Grace, LTD* (2019). This Neo or Western noir focuses on a hardscrabble pastor named Pa (Sir Ben Kingsley) who comes upon a grifter played by Jimmi Simpson, best known for his turn on HBO's *Westworld* (2016). Simpson's grifter becomes embroiled in a plot to steal from Pa, only to discover that Pa is not at all what he seems. Steve Conrad and Bruce Terris, both fresh off the success of the idiosyncratic spy drama *Patriot* (2015), created the show. Terris explained their approach to *Collider.com*: " Oftentimes in noir, it seems like the characters are a bit one-dimensional. There's the bad guy and the good guy, and the evil guy. I've known Steve for twenty years, and he's really been my mentor, as a writer, and what he really taught me, which my experience as a human backs up, is that there really are no one-dimensional characters because there are no one-dimensional people." The show lasted for one season on Epix. *Perpetual Grace, LTD* made use of the top-floor pool at La Fonda to mimic a resort in Mexico. Most of the show was shot primarily around Santa Fe. For more on La Fonda, check out the Page to Screen tour on page 4.

To reach the next stop, head out the corner of La Fonda and walk through the plaza to the Plaza Café (54 Lincoln Avenue, Santa Fe, NM, 87501; 505-982-1664, plazacafesantafe.com). You'll see it just across the street on the other side of the plaza. Here, actor Anton Yelchin saw demons in a fictionalized version of the Plaza Café. Most guests will see enchiladas and tortilla soup.

Just feet from the center of the Santa Fe Plaza itself, the Plaza Café serves New Mexican food classics and is a staple for the film industry. Yelchin, who also starred in the reboot of the *Star Trek* (2009) franchise, played Odd, a short order cook in the Plaza Café and the titular character in *Odd Thomas* (2013). Odd has the ability to see both dead people and demons, which reliably arrive as the omens of death and tragedy. He does battle with these creatures across a number of familiar Santa Fe landmarks, including the Plaza Café, several nearby street intersections, and the Santa Fe Place Mall on the southern end of town.

The film was directed by Stephen Sommers, who rose to fame on *The Mummy* (1999) reboot films that starred Brendan Fraser. The films were massive hits, reinvigorating interest in a film franchise that had roots in 1932. Sommers enjoyed a decade of commercial success at the box office, helming the Hugh Jackman starrer *Van Helsing* (2004) and *GI Joe: The Rise of the Cobra* (2009). For *Odd Thomas,* Sommers had a smaller budget to work with than his previous blockbusters, but the film had a budding star in Yelchin, notable supporting actors in Willem Dafoe and Gugu Mbatha-Raw, and established source material from Dean Koontz's novel of the same name.

Actor Nick Nolte was haunted not by ghouls, but by his old electorate as he played a former United States President, struggling with his legacy in retirement. As President Richard Graves, Nolte took frequent breakfasts at a local diner, where he befriends a waitress played by Callie Hernandez, who helps him touch base with the everyday citizen. After reflecting, President

Anton Yelchin behind the grill in *Odd Thomas* (2013). Courtesy of Image Entertainment.

Graves decides to rock the boat by redoing some of his mistakes while in office and challenging the Conservative establishment. In the process, he also manages to butt heads with a burgeoning politician, his wife, played by actress Sela Ward.

Graves ran for several seasons on Epix and shot largely in greater Albuquerque, with occasional sojourns to Santa Fe. The show's creator, Joshua Michael Stern, previously shot *Swing Vote* (2008) starring Kevin Costner in Belen, making *Graves* the second political comedy he brought to the state.

The real Plaza Café has endured some drama. A local institution that bills itself as the oldest restaurant on the plaza, it nearly burned down to the ground after a kitchen fire in 2010. The damage made the café a perfect filming location for *Odd Thomas*, but the restaurant had to be largely remodeled afterward. It's now a dependable destination for New Mexican favorites served alongside Greek salads. The restaurant has a second location in southern Santa Fe that serves similar food.

From the Plaza Café, walk across West Palace Avenue to the New Mexico Museum of Art (107 West Palace Avenue, Santa Fe, NM, 87501; 505-476-5072, nmartmuseum.org) Built in 1917 as one of the first structures to integrate the budding Spanish Pueblo Revival style, the façade of the museum integrates the designs of historic missions at Acoma and Laguna Pueblos and architect Isaac H. Raap's prior work at the Panama-California Exposition in 1915. The event at San Diego's Balboa Park helped bring New Mexico's cultures to the world. When it opened, the Museum of Fine Arts served as a meeting place for the burgeoning arts scene just then sprouting in Santa Fe. The museum has since been expanded and retitled to remove the word "fine," because their collection includes a broader array of art.

The museum is probably best known as the home of high art, but it has also hosted some lowbrow moviemaking. *And God Created Woman* (1988), a sexual romp in which Rebecca De Mornay plays an ex con, shot a pivotal final sequence at the museum. De Mornay, as Robin Shea, manages to sneak on stage at a fundraiser for gubernatorial candidate James Tiernan, played by Frank Langella. There, with some wicked wailing and a rad tube top, Shea sets her world right.

The film was ostensibly a remake of the 1956 flick of the same name. The original starred Brigitte Bardot as a wily temptress stuck in a love triangle between two brothers. *And God Created Woman* established Bardot as an international sensation, and, it might be argued, moved the sexual liberation movement into a new age. At the very least, the film set up Roger Vadim as a director who could advance the career of young actors like Bardot. The updated rendition returned Vadim but not much else. The remake's plot did not follow that of the original except that the heroine leveraged her sexual prowess into a fight for freedom in both films. In a press kit recorded interview now posted online, De Mornay said she took the part because she believed that it held an "interesting, unorthodox view of feminism."

The movie also had a lot of 1980s glam rock. De Mornay even practiced the bass for months before shooting started in order to look more realistic during the musical numbers, which were choreographed by Kenny Ortega of *Dirty Dancing* fame. *And God Created Woman* also shot on the plaza and at the Randall Davey Audubon Center & Sanctuary and the Santa Fe Opera, among other locations.

The New Mexico Museum of the Arts as it appears in *And God Created Woman* (1988). Courtesy of Lionsgate.

After checking out the museum, make a right on Palace Avenue. Go across the street to the Delgado House at 124 Palace Avenue. The historic building, constructed in 1890 using telltale Territorial stylings including the Italian-inspired portico and ornate balcony, once belonged to the merchant and trader Felipe Delgado. Famed architect John Gaw Meem later purchased it for conservation. The building was used as a lawyer's office in *News of the World* (2020). The film is adapted from the novella of the same name by Paulette Jiles and follows Tom Hanks as a former Confederate soldier, General Jefferson Kyle Kidd, who travels the West after the Civil War to read the news aloud. Along the way, he comes to the defense of a German-speaking girl who is caught between her adopted Native American home, her blood relatives, and frontier hooligans. The film was directed by Paul Greengrass, who rose to prominence on the strength of the Jason Bourne spy thrillers. He directed *The Bourne Supremacy* (2004), *The Bourne Ultimatum* (2007) and the self-titled *Jason Bourne* (2016). His success with the franchise made him one of the most in-demand action auteurs in the industry.

News of the World showcased Greengrass's penchant for propulsion with a stirring shootout, a runaway wagon sequence, and a dust storm, all filmed around greater Santa Fe. The Western, though, was also punctuated by quiet and sincere moments and Kidd's search for a family after the trauma and tragedy of the Civil War. Not surprisingly, Hanks is heartfelt in his search for a new family in the far west. As of press time, the Delgado House was occupied by the Victory Contemporary Gallery (505-983-8589; victorycontemporary.com). After you've had a look inside, go back toward the Museum of Art and up Palace Avenue.

Here, go past the portal for the Palace of the Governors and take a left on Washington Avenue, stay on the palace side of the street, and you'll run directly into a Santa Fe literary magnate bronzed discreetly on the sidewalk. That's Fray Angélico Chávez, the early New Mexico historian and intellectual and the namesake of the history library right in front of him. Feel free to greet father Chávez before continuing about half a block to the small plaza on the left and a steak joint called the Bull Ring (150 Washington Avenue, Santa Fe, NM; 505-983-3328, santafebullring.com).

The swank restaurant makes for a culinary change of pace to the New Mexican and Mexican restaurants that dominate the area. It also made frequent appearances in the second season of *Waco* as a gathering place for lawyers. Giovanni Ribisi, as Dan Cogdell, and his team, defending the survivors of the siege at Waco, convene regularly at the restaurant to go over their plans. Things take a twist when they eventually realize they may not have been the only people in the restaurant interested in the case. Get your prime cut on, then head back to Palace Avenue and hang a left.

The next two buildings on this walk have pronounced portals and hidden interior plazas. Both harken back to the Santa Fe Trail and the early to mid-1800s. The first building you'll pass once belonged to Antoine Robidoux, a fur trapper who also worked as the interpreter for United States Brigadier General Stephen Watts Kearny, the man most responsible for the conquest of California. The home was later owned by State Supreme Court Justice L. Bradford Prince. Next door, Sena Plaza, is about the same age as the first. Both buildings are among the older surviving homes in Santa Fe and played an even greater role in history a century after they were built.

Unassuming Santa Fe was at the forefront of international events when it had a small part in the Manhattan Project. The brainchild of physicist J. Robert Oppenheimer, the Manhattan Project, under the greater umbrella of Project Y, was a covert American operation launched during World War II with the lofty intention of developing a weapon that could harness the power of the atom. Oppenheimer chose to place his labs in isolated Los Alamos, knowing that secrecy was paramount to success and safety. The road to Los Alamos, though, began in Santa Fe.

To reach the lab, personnel with appropriate clearance had to check in at a nondescript location just feet from the Santa Fe Plaza. At 109 East Palace Avenue, a secretary greeted those traveling to the lab and checked them in, issued them security badges and then ushered them on to a rough, nearly forty-mile drive, to "the Hill." There's a marker pointing the way to the small plaza where the office stood. In case that wasn't obvious enough, you might also spot signage for a coffee shop called Oppie's, which wasn't operating at press time. Nearby, a plaque marks the location of the pickup, but the Los Alamos National Labs hasn't used the location since 1963.

Two of Santa Fe's signature restaurants are also on this block. The Shed (113½ East Palace Ave. Santa Fe, NM, 87501; 505-982-9030, sfshed.com) might be the most indispensable of Santa Fe's eateries, famed for its New Mexican selections, its garlic bread, and its ambiance in the historic Trujillo, Prince Building. Next door, La Casa Sena has charming seating in the Sena Building's historic courtyard and a Mediterranean-inspired menu but was temporarily closed at press time.

Make your way past the cathedral on East Palace Ave. Before hitting Paseo de Peralta, you'll spot the Drury Plaza Hotel on your right. The hotel, formerly a hospital, reportedly has at least one ghoulish resident. Guests have recounted sightings of a young boy who knocks on the door of room 311.

The basement of the building is also filled with ghosts. Once a sanatorium, it's no surprise that a few grim incidents have occurred on the site. For more on the hotel, check out the Santa Funky walking tour on page 56.

Continue on East Palace Avenue several blocks and then cross Paseo de Peralta to reach La Posada de Santa Fe Resort & Spa (330 East Palace Avenue, Santa Fe, NM 87501; 505-986-0000, laposadadesantafe.com).

The historic hotel named their on-site restaurant after Julia Schuster, who married the merchant Abraham Staab and moved to New Mexico Territory with him. In 1882, he built her a sprawling, French Second Empire–style home, where she raised a large family. Julia died in 1896, then purportedly returned as an apparition eight decades later. Several employees claimed to have seen "a translucent woman with white upswept hair and a black Victorian dress standing near a fireplace." Elsewhere in the hotel, flower pots and chandeliers moved on their own. Julia's old room, now Suite 100, is said to be one of her favorite spots.

If you'd like her company, the hotel offers a two-night ghost package, but Julia sightings are not guaranteed. For more on Julia herself, you can read *American Ghost: A Family's Haunted Past in the Desert Southwest* written by Staab's descendant Hannah Nordhaus. The book goes in to detail on Julia's experience as a mail-order bride and her legendary afterlife.

Or, you can wait for her at the hotel's bar, The Staab House, named after the pioneer family. The historic bar with elegant leather seating and Victorian vibes is worth a stop and is part of the official Santa Fe Margarita Trail. After you enjoy one of The Staab House's signature cocktails, you can head back to Paseo de Peralta and hang a left. Proceed up Paseo de Peralta to Alameda and make a right.

Along Alameda, you'll spot the Santa Fe River. The banks of this seasonal stream are one place you might see La Llorona. Sightings of this dreadful phantasm, though, are common throughout the Latin American world. The wailing widow haunts bodies of waters, mourning the loss of the children she drowned. Her story makes a convenient warning to all young people who like to stray from home—she might well attack if children wander too close to rivers. Although several different forms of La Llorona legends are prevalent throughout the Southwest, she has a firm hold on the mythology of the Land of Enchantment and is frequently the subject of conversation all over northern New Mexico. La Llorona has also been the subject of at least several films including a recent horror film called, not surprisingly, *The Curse of La Llorona* (2019). The film shot largely in Los Angeles.

Keep your children close and make another right on Old Santa Fe Trail.

Here you'll find a supernatural story that is not terrifying, but miraculous—in particular, a staircase inside the neo-Gothically accented Loretto Chapel (207 Old Santa Fe Trail, Santa Fe, NM, 87501; 505-982-0092, lorettochapel.com) that defies both gravity and expectations.

Designed for the Sisters of Loretto, the chapel construction began in 1874, with a plan that incorporated elements of the Saint-Chapelle in Paris, known for its Gothic buttresses and stained glass windows. The Loretto Chapel was made of hewn sandstone and a volcanic rock called scoria. The chapel featured pronounced tunnel vaults and stained-glass windows imported from the DuBois studio in France. Despite its magnificence, the chapel didn't have a staircase to the choir loft and the architect assigned to the project died before he could install it. This seemingly minor problem required a difficult solution.

The sisters needed a way to access the choir loft that didn't take up floor space in the compact cathedral, making a typical staircase unfeasible. They prayed to Saint Joseph, the patron saint of carpenters, for nine days. According to lore, a mysterious woodworker arrived shortly thereafter. He had only a few rudimentary tools with him, but used them to build a spiral staircase with thirty-three steps and wooden pegs fastening it together. The staircase defied the rules of physics. To add to the mystery, the woodworker who made it purportedly disappeared as suddenly as he had arrived.

The story, now a part of Santa Fe's mythology, was enough to become the basis of a 1998 made-for-television movie called, not surprisingly, *The Staircase*. Barbara Hershey and William Petersen, later famed for his long run on *CSI: Crime Scene Investigation*, starred in the film. Petersen played Joad, a

Loretto Chapel's miraculous staircase. Photograph by Karol M., Wikimedia Commons.

mysterious vagabond hired by Hershey's character Mother Madalyn to work on the staircase. To complicate matters, Madalyn is in failing health and sees the chapel as one of her last great works for the church. By contracting the mysterious Joad to work on the stairs, she also causes regional consternation, provoking the local architect. He vows to stop Joad at all costs, even if it means violence. Most of the film shot at the ranches near Santa Fe.

The Albuquerque-based television show *In Plain Sight* also shot at the chapel. The show featured Mary McCormack as a U.S. Marshal assigned to the Federal Witness Security Program in New Mexico. The show had solid ratings and ran for five seasons on the USA network.

Almost as long running, the CW's reimagination of the sci-fi drama *Roswell* shot four seasons in New Mexico. The original show was adapted from the young adult novel *Roswell High* by Melinda Metz, published in the late 1990s. The series enjoyed a brief stint on two networks before it was canceled in 2001. *Roswell, New Mexico* (2019) modernized the show, introducing themes of racism and migration. The pilot shot in Albuquerque and after receiving the green light, the series moved to Santa Fe.

The change of venue added a new dynamic, executive producer, and showrunner. Christopher Hollier said in an interview with *Assignment X*: "It's actually helping us deepen our own mythology. Carina [Adly MacKenzie, co-showrunner] and I spent a lot of time over the summer looking at what actual things exist in Santa Fe and New Mexico for us to pull from. There's so much of the Manhattan Project, so much science that was actually done by our government, in that place, that we've looked at a lot of that and blended that with the cultures that lived there."

The show used the Loretto Chapel several times. It also shot extensively in Las Vegas (check out the chapter on Las Vegas for more details). The Loretto Chapel was deconsecrated in 1968, so that it could become a permanent museum. It's open for visitation for a small fee. (Five dollars for adults at press time.) An audio presentation at the chapel explains the history of its creation.

According to some, the ghost of a nun still inhabits the hotel attached to the chapel. Once a teacher and a member of the Order of the Sisters of Loretto, Sister George died in 1976 and reappeared at the hotel shortly afterward. She has a predilection for prank phone calls and, according to at least one report, cigars. The Inn & Spa at Loretto (211 Old Santa Fe Trail, Santa Fe, NM 87501; 505-988-5531, hotelloretto.com) is also a favorite for productions in the area.

Selected Filmography

Arthur, Karen, dir. *The Staircase*. CBS, 1998. TV movie.

Conrad, Steve, and Bruce Terris, creators. *Perpetual Grace, LTD*. MGM Television, 2019–2020. TV series.

Dowdle, John Eric and Drew, creators. *Waco: The Aftermath*. Showtime Network, 2023. TV series.

MacKenzie, Carina Adly, creator. *Roswell, New Mexico*. The CW, 2019. TV series.

Maples, David, creator. *In Plain Sight*. USA Network, 2008–2012. TV series

Sommers, Stephen, dir. *Odd Thomas*. Image Entertainment, 2013. Film.

Stern, Joshua Michael, creator. *Graves*. Epix, 2016–2017. TV series.

Vadim, Roger, dir. *And God Created Woman*. Lionsgate, 1987. Film.

TOUR 3

Santa Fe Trail—Road Trips

Start: Market Street and Manhattan

Distance: 1.4 miles

Time: 55 minutes

Highlights: Bert's Burger Bowl, the Santa Fe County Administration Complex, Georgia O'Keeffe Museum, Palace Restaurant, Santa Fe Scottish Rite Center

Parking: Metered street parking on Catron Street or Jefferson Street

Beyond the rhythmic beat of Native American drums and flutes, there's another pervasive soundtrack in Santa Fe—the rumbling of automobile and motorcycle engines. New Mexico is the home of the Low Rider and Route 66. The state is filled with car culture. Route 66, though, was far from the first famous thoroughfare through the region.

In the post-colonial era, Santa Fe is well known as the end of the trail that bore its name. "The Great Prairie Highway" ran from Missouri to New Mexico and served as a major conduit for trade and travel from 1821 until roughly 1880, although its decline began decades earlier. Regardless, the legacy of the trail has continued.

Route 66 from Chicago to Los Angeles arrived decades later. Officially created in 1926, the 2,400-mile corridor began its life as little more than a loosely connected series of county roads. Parts of it remained unpaved for more than a decade. The route also meandered through rural areas so farmers could ship out their crops. The "Mother Road" came to prominence just as the rest of the country was plunged into the Great Depression. Hundreds of thousands of Americans affected by drought or lack of opportunity headed west to California. After World War II,

Bert's Burger Bowl as it appears in *Two-Lane Blacktop* (1971).
Courtesy of Universal Pictures.

as car culture grabbed the nation, the cross-country road hit its stride as a destination for adventurers and travelers.

Route 66 left a physical and stylistic imprint on New Mexico. Because the road wound its way across the state, period gas stations, motels, and diners can be found in places like Tucumcari, Pecos, and Gallup. The route also traversed Albuquerque and Santa Fe. Albuquerque's Central Avenue is still decorated by neon signs from the heyday of the road. In Santa Fe, Route 66 cut through downtown, near La Fonda. Because Santa Fe codified its architectural style, the remnants of the old thoroughfare are not as visible as elsewhere in the state.

Director Monte Hellman chose to make his muscle car, road-trip flick on actual segments of Route 66, opting for those stretches over budget-friendly rural Los Angeles. Hellman grew up in New York, was educated in California, and then was mentored by B-film impresario Roger Corman. In the mid-1960s, Hellman directed several Westerns written by and starring a young actor named Jack Nicholson. A few years later, Nicholson found his stride, and national attention, with a brief role in director Dennis Hopper's cross-country cult classic, *Easy Rider* (1969).

Made for roughly $400,000, Hopper's *Easy Rider* grossed $20 million. It was also a cultural phenomenon that spurred Hollywood interest in more youth-focused films. Although Hellman's *Two-Lane Blacktop* (1971) had a production budget of $850,000, Universal Studios saw an opportunity to replicate the success of *Easy Rider* in both the script and the indie darling director.

The first stop on this tour is one of the real-life locations that Hellman used for the film, a Mexican restaurant called Santa Fe Bees (235 North Guadalupe, Santa Fe, NM 87501; 505-954-1008, santafebeesrestaurant.com).

Before it was Santa Fe Bees, the building was home to Bert's Burger Bowl. This hamburger counter–style restaurant was something of a local institution until it shuttered in 2015 after more than sixty years in business. The restaurant was famed for its late-night sandwiches and green chile cheeseburgers. Bert's Burger Bowl got prime placement in *Two-Lane Blacktop*.

Hellman wanted his road warriors to have an air of authenticity and shied away from practiced actors. Instead, he cast musicians James Taylor and the Beach Boys' Dennis Wilson to star in the film, as well as model Laurie Bird. Of the lead cast, only Warren Oates had logged significant thespian time. Wilson and Taylor, though, had more than enough presence and confidence to fill up the screen. If Route 66 was already filled with some of the hippest people around, Taylor and Wilson were the literal rock stars of the road as they cruised across the nation.

Along the way, they stop at popular hangouts to show off their superior steel and impress the crowd. At one such hangout—Bert's Burger Bowl—they challenge a local blowhard to a race, only to clean his clock and take the man's pink slip. The local sucker was played by the film's screenwriter Rudy Wurlitzer. A novelist by trade, Wurlitzer rewrote the original script for the film. In the final draft, none of the characters are named implying an existential and replaceable nature for these All-American characters.

When it premiered in 1971, critics had a mixed reaction to the film. While *Esquire* magazine ran an extensive spread on *Two-Lane Blacktop,* even publishing much of the script, some critics bumped on the film's barren landscapes and sparse dialogue. After a few weeks in theaters, the studio pulled the release. It didn't take long, though, for French cinephiles to discover the movie and transform it into a cult classic. For his part, Hellman became a hero of indie filmmaking and largely stayed in that lane (play on words intended) throughout the rest of his long career.

The film also placed Hellman in "director jail." Because of his unorthodox decisions like not giving the script to star James Taylor, and the film's poor performance at the box office, Hellman didn't work for a major studio as a director for decades. Lew Wasserman, Hollywood's formative agent and renowned king, purportedly disliked the film so much that he single-handedly buried it. More likely, though, the film simply failed to live up to its marketing ideals and fell flat at the box office.

Grab a taco and rev up your walking engine: this walk continues up Catron Street.

Catron Street takes a circuitous route toward the Plaza. Its namesake, Thomas Benton Catron, was a New Mexican lawyer and politician who used his influence and power to acquire huge tracts of land in the New Mexico Territory in the late-nineteenth century. Catron became one of the best-known members of the shadowy Santa Fe Ring, a loose consortium of politicians and investors who commandeered control of the territory. Famously, the ring's subsidiaries in southern New Mexico battled Billy the Kid and his Regulators.

Catron Street goes past a café and a school before it becomes Federal Place. On your right, you'll notice a rather large Pueblo-style office that houses the Santa Fe County Administration Complex. Finished in 2019, the building replaced the Old Judicial Complex.

Originally built as a junior high school in 1937, the Old Judicial Complex fell into disuse in 2013, but became an available and convenient setting for scenes of law and order. The made-for-television, true crime and history story *Outlaw Prophet* (2014) shot several court scenes inside the abandoned building. The film tells the story of Fundamentalist Church of Jesus Christ of Latter-day Saints leader Warren Jeffs. After assuming control of his community, Jeffs illicitly arranged the marriages of underage women and subsequently went on the run from the FBI, before he was captured and tried for his crimes. The film was based on actual events.

Outlaw Prophet starred Tony Goldwyn as Jeffs. The grandson of famed film producer and studio executive, Samuel Goldwyn, Tony Goldwyn might be best known for playing President Fitzgerald Grant III in the long-running ABC show *Scandal* (2012), although his career has lasted almost four decades.

Continue down Grant Avenue to the corner of Johnson Street. On your right, you'll spot the Georgia O'Keeffe Museum (217 Johnson Street, Santa Fe, NM, 87501; 505-946-1000, okeeffemuseum.org). Among the newer entries to Santa Fe's museum scene, the Georgia O'Keeffe Museum opened in 1997 with the express intent of showing off the works of the iconic artist.

The museum makes a cameo in *Breaking Bad* in the eleventh episode of season 3 as the show's second lead Jesse Pinkman takes his girlfriend, Jane, for something of a field trip. Jesse's attempt at a loving relationship, though, is short-lived. Jane is murdered just an episode later. Their conversation at the museum eventually symbolized their brief moment of happiness. For more on *Breaking Bad,* check out the section on Albuquerque, where the show was based.

The Georgia O'Keeffe Museum showcases a representative collection of O'Keeffe's paintings, background on her life, and temporary exhibitions. Once you've enjoyed the museum's offerings, follow your steps back on Grant Avenue and make a right to West Palace Avenue.

Just to your left, you'll spot the former Palace Restaurant, now Palace Prime (142 West Palace Avenue, Santa Fe, NM 87501; 505-919-9935, palaceprimesf.com). This velour-lined, mood-lit bar and eatery claims to be more than a century old. The exterior made a brief appearance in *Longmire* in the second episode of season 3 as a restaurant frequented by the titular character's wife, Martha.

Deceased before the continuity of the show begins, the mystery surrounding Martha's death fuels the secondary story of the first half of the show's run. In a series of flashbacks that reveal the circumstances of her untimely demise, Martha's body is discovered in a dumpster in an alley. Although dressed up to look more urban, that backstreet is actually Burro Alley just a few feet back down Palace Avenue at the intersection with Sandoval Street.

About one block long, the passageway is punctuated by a modernist-style statue of a cord-carrying donkey. The burro represents one of many tasked with bringing wood down from the Sangre de Cristo Mountains. After their trips were completed, the donkeys were often left to congregate in this alley, hence their immortalization in bronze. The alley winds up at The Lensic Performing Arts Center (211 West San Francisco Street, Santa Fe, NM, 87501; 505-988-1234, lensic.org).

The Lensic's marquee is hard to miss among the Pueblo Revival building of Santa Fe. Financed by a local merchant who dreamed of elevating Santa Fe's artistic prowess, the Lensic was initially constructed in 1931. This new theater, built on a site once made famous by the nineteenth-century entrepreneur, gambler, entertainer and hotelier, María Gertrudis Barceló, known as Doña Tules, incorporated Mexican baroque stylings and a rather grand façade. The theater was remodeled in 2001 and now has a robust schedule of concerts, lectures, simulcasts and films.

The 1940 Errol Flynn film *The Santa Fe Trail* premiered at the Lensic that year. Amazingly, the film had little to do with its namesake. Flynn starred as Confederate General Jeb Stuart and Ronald Reagan appeared as George Armstrong Custer. Olivia de Havilland also starred in the film.

The love triangle story had little to do with history and shot mostly on film ranches in California.

The Lensic also hosted the premier of *The Milagro Beanfield War* (1988). Based on the book of the same name by New Mexico author John Nichols, the film told the story of a fictionalized northern New Mexican community where a real estate developer threatens traditional ways of life by hijacking the local water source. Out of desperation and frustration, a farmer breaks a waterpipe, allowing his beanfields to flood. This inadvertent act of defiance quickly brings tensions to bear in Milagro.

Directed by Robert Redford, the film shot mostly on the scenic High Road to Taos in the small town of Truchas. Production delays, cold weather, and even a rumored affair between cast members put the film over budget. When finally released, it met with tepid reviews. In the years since, though, the film has ascended to a cult classic sort of following. For more on the film, check out Nichols's recollection of the process in his entertaining essay "Night of the Living Beanfield: How an Unsuccessful Cult Novel Became an Unsuccessful Cult Film in Only Fourteen Years, Eleven Nervous Breakdowns, and $20 Million" in his collection of essays *Dancing on the Stones*, published in 2000.

While premieres are not regular events at the Lensic, yearly film festivals and event screenings are on their calendar. Catch one if your timing is fortuitous. Then, walk past the Lensic and cross Sandoval Street to the Eldorado Hotel & Spa. One of Santa Fe's grander hotels, the Eldorado pops up briefly in the Michael Keaton and Geena Davis romantic comedy *Speechless* (1994). The two 1990s power players depict speechwriters on opposing campaigns who fall for each other while they tour New Mexico with their respective senatorial candidates. Their rivalry, though, puts a damper on their blossoming relationship, as does the appearance of a dashing Christopher Reeves as Davis's former lover. The film also shot in Las Vegas and at La Fonda Hotel.

The movie marked director Ron Underwood's second go round on a comedy in New Mexico. His first film in the state, *City Slickers* (1991), proved a genre-bending hit. The movie's most iconic scenes were filmed in and near Ghost Ranch just a few miles north of Abiquíu, New Mexico. *Speechless,* though, didn't quite hit funny bones in the same way.

Renny Harlin, another prolific director, produced the film as a part of a years' long collaboration with his creative and romantic partner, Davis. The two moved on to make *Cutthroat Island* (1995), one of the most notorious bombs of the 1990s. The film put a temporary hold on Davis's career, although their successive film *Long Kiss Goodnight* (1996) became something of a cult classic. Harlin and Davis were spotted together in downtown Santa Fe, bringing a little bit of tabloid chic to the city.

If you're not staying at the Eldorado Hotel, you can still stop in for a drink at the sleek Agave Restaurant and Lounge (309 W San Francisco Street, Santa Fe, NM 87501; 505-988-4455, eldoradohotel.com/eat_drink/agave_lounge/), which has a distinctly urban feel. Afterward, you can retrace your steps past the Lensic, *or* you can take a left on Sandoval and another immediate left on Grant Avenue. Walk two blocks and look across the street, and you'll spot the Santa Fe Community Convention Center. Make a right up Marcy for a few examples of unique Santa Fe art.

On your left, *27 Rio Grande Cutthroat Trout* by sculptor Collette Hosmer features large granite fish heads popping out of a granite river. The statue makes a fun obstacle course for kids and a photo opportunity for adults. You can join the many visitors who tagged their social post with some version of "#swimmingupstream."

Less than a block up the sidewalk is an equally distinctive statue of a local hero, Sergeant 1st Class Leroy Petry of the 75th Ranger Regiment. Sergeant Petry served two tours in Iraq and six in Afghanistan. Petry shielded his fellow soldiers from a grenade and saved several lives in Afghanistan but lost his hand in the process. For his sacrifice and heroism, Petry received a Purple Heart and a Medal of Honor for his service, among many other decorations.

Proceed up West Marcy to Lincoln Avenue and across Federal Park at South Federal Place.

Note the Gothic Revival courthouse adjacent to the Federal Park. The stone building was originally intended to be the territorial capitol when construction began in 1850. Federal funding, though, ran low, and the structure remained unfinished for decades until it was finally completed in 1883. It was never used as a capitol building but instead as housing during New Mexico's Tertio-Centennial Celebration, marking the region's 333rd birthday, and then, later, as a part of the U.S. District Court.

You can spot the courthouse in the third episode of the second season of *Longmire*. During a family subplot, Walt Longmire's daughter, Cady, goes in search of her mother's killer and is recognized by a friend. The courthouse is visible behind them when they meet. The courthouse returns in the third episode of the sixth season of the show, making an official-looking backdrop as Walt Longmire and his lawyer discuss a trial that endangers the sheriff's future. Take a stroll through the park and then head to the stoplight on Paseo de Peralta to cross over to the unmistakable building on the other side.

Hard to camouflage in real life, the Southwestern pink stucco Santa Fe Scottish Rite Center (463 Paseo de Peralta, Santa Fe, NM 87504; 505-982-4414, santafescottishrite.org) appears frequently in shows that use Santa Fe. Completed in 1912, the center showcases Moorish architecture borrowed heavily from the gatehouse at the Alhambra in Spain. The famed Spanish edifice actually provided the namesake for the theater inside the center.

In the Epix television show *Perpetual Grace, LTD.*, the building was decorated as a British orphanage where Sir Ben Kingsley's character Pa spent part of his youth before moving to the United States. You can also look for the center to pop up in the Megan Fox film *Passion Play* (2010) and Tina Fey's *Whiskey Tango Foxtrot* (2016).

Based on the memoirs of war correspondent Kim Barker, *The Taliban Shuffle: Strange Days in Afghanistan and Pakistan, Whiskey Tango Foxtrot* follows a journalist attempting to find her way through fighting in the Middle East. Part comedy, part war drama, and part historical recreation, the film was mostly shot around Albuquerque with occasional forays into the mountains and to Santa Fe.

Whiskey Tango Foxtrot became one of a number of war films to substitute New Mexico for the Middle East. Look carefully and you'll recognize New Mexico's pinion-juniper forests in films like *Lone Survivor* (2013), *12 Strong* (2018), and *Ghosted* (2023). Most of these films gravitated toward the mountains and mesas near Albuquerque or Las Cruces.

Take a look around the center, if open, and then return to the courthouse and continue back down Washington Avenue until it terminates at the plaza. The Santa Fe Trail ended its journey here as well. A carved stone monument on the Palace of the Governors side of the plaza commemorates the heyday of the trail.

If you'd like to see what the plaza looked like circa 1980, check out the comedy *Second Thoughts* (1983). The film opens on the plaza with a street musician jamming on the harmonica. In the background, you'll spot the Woolworth's department store, which closed in 1988, and is now a Five & Dime. The convenience/souvenir store opened in 1998 and established a reputation for their Frito Pie, a bag of Fritos topped with chili, cheese, and onions. Food critic and traveler Antony Bourdain visited the store to try this New Mexican classic during the fifteenth episode of the fourth season of *Parts Unknown*. Bourdain said that the combination of Fritos and chili was "as American as apple pie or the Manhattan Project and nearly as deadly." After the show premiered, though, Bourdain's team apologized for his terse criticism and walked back his rather harsh review in which he likened the snack to "crap in a bag." The convenience and souvenir store was also the subject of a documentary released in 2023 entitled *A Five and Dime Story* that recounted the history of the business.

Lucie Arnaz, the star of *Second Thoughts*, took after her parents—Lucille Ball and Desi Arnaz—as an actor. Ball also starred in a film that unfolded in New Mexico and prefigured Lucie by about thirty years. *Fancy Pants* starred Ball and Bob Hope as an American actor impersonating an English butler,

Lobby card for *Fancy Pants* (1950). Courtesy of the Paul Andrew Hutton Collection and Paramount Pictures.

who is sent West to join Ball. Hope's character soon becomes embroiled in multiple charades, his true story threatening to come to the light.

Lucie Arnaz never reached the lofty fame of her mother. She did, however, have a moment of stardom. After starring in the hit remake of *The Jazz Singer* (1980), this one featuring Neil Diamond succeeding Al Jolson in the spotlight, Lucie had a number of offers for her next part. She considered *Poltergeist* (1982), but then turned it down, believing that *Second Thoughts* offered a better opportunity as an actor. The comedy, though, was something of a bomb, attempting to mesh humor with an abortion story.

The plaza also cameos in *Powwow Highway* (1989). The film starred A Martinez and Gary Farmer as two Cheyenne men living in a community in flux. Playing Buddy Red Bow, Martinez is actively engaged in resisting a construction project on his home reservation. Then he gets word that his sister has been detained in faraway Santa Fe. To make the trip, Red Bow needs a car, and his old friend Philbert Bono, played by Gary Farmer, happens to have one. Bono, though, is in the midst of a spiritual reawakening, and the two men spend much of their trip arguing. Nothing on their haphazard journey goes according to plan, but they still make it to Santa Fe.

Based on the book of the same name by David Seals, the film met with some critical fanfare, winning the Filmmaker's Trophy at the 1989 Sundance Film Festival. The film also helped launch the careers of Native actors Wes Studi and Graham Greene. After shooting wrapped, Studi, Farmer, and director Jonathan Wacks became Santa Fe regulars.

Martinez returned to Santa Fe as a community magnate in *Longmire*. Although constantly at odds with Sheriff Longmire, Martinez's Jacob Nighthorse is an important leader in the local Native American community and has hopes of building a casino called the Four Arrows. Nighthorse refuses to be thwarted. He cuts some unsavory deals and keeps dangerous company in order to preserve the future of his casino. This serious entrepreneur is a long way from the comical character that Martinez played in *Powwow Highway*.

In an earlier buddy-road-trip flick, Dean Martin and Jerry Lewis zipped across the country to settle a debt and meet the stars in Los Angeles in the appropriately titled *Hollywood or Bust* (1956). As they race across states toward California, accompanied by Pat Crowley, the two zoom past the Santa Fe Plaza while singing a ditty about uranium and Geiger counters.

The 1960s television hit, *Route 66*, shot three episodes in and around Santa Fe. The plaza, La Fonda, and the Cathedral Basilica of St. Francis de Assisi are all visible in the show's first season. Starring heartthrob George Maharis as Buz Murdock and Martin Milner as Tod Stiles, *Route 66* follows a set of friends as they crisscross the country in a shiny Corvette. Along the way, they bump into more than their fair share of trouble as they witness

Looking over Santa Fe in *Route 66* (1960). Courtesy of CBS Television.

the rise of a post-war America. The show shot all over the West, sometimes on the actual Route 66. In the twenty-sixth episode of the first season, "A Skill for Hunting," the two leads bump into a drunkard who is hunting a doe. They foil his effort and soon find themselves with a dangerous enemy who tries to take his revenge on the boys.

In addition to their shooting downtown, the show also filmed in the hills around Santa Fe. The twenty-seventh episode of the first season, "Trap at Cordova," actually filmed at the Rio Arriba County town for which it was named and in Santa Fe. Our two heroes get involved in a roadside ploy involving an overturned wagon that would have been at home on the Old Santa Fe Trail. The trap was designed to ensnare an empathetic and learned individual who would be willing to stay and teach in the small and isolated

Cordova. Their mischievous methods run into a serious problem when they stop Buz and Tod. In addition to seeing the small Hispano village of Cordova, you can also spot the Bataan Memorial Building in Santa Fe in the background (more on that building in the Page to Screen tour on page 4).

The show ran for four seasons airing more than one hundred episodes on CBS and drew in an impressive array of guest stars like William Shatner, Ron Howard, Robert Redford, and Julie Newmar. Many of these actors appeared in the show before they had made their reputations. Some of them surfaced in the meaty parts that the show set up in episodic narratives taking place in far-flung parts of the United States. Ultimately, only three episodes shot in New Mexico, although the state has deep ties to the legacy of the historical Route 66.

Selected Filmography

Baldwin, Hunt, and John Coveny, creators. *Longmire*. A+E Networks, 2012–2017. TV series.

Ficarra, Glenn, and John Requa, dirs. *Whiskey Tango Foxtrot*. Paramount Pictures, 2016. Film.

Hellman, Monte, dir. *Two-Lane Blacktop*. Universal Pictures, 1971. DVD.

Hopper, Dennis, and Peter Fonda, dirs. *Easy Rider*. Columbia Pictures, 1969. DVD.

Leonard, Herbert and Stirling Siliphant, creators. *Route 66*. CBS, 1960–1964. TV series.

Range, Gabriel, dir. *Outlaw Prophet: Warren Jeffs*. Lifetime Television, 2014. TV movie.

Redford, Robert, dir. *The Milagro Beanfield War*. Universal Pictures, 1988. Film.

Tashlin, Frank, dir. *Hollywood or Bust*. Paramount, 1956. Film.

Turman, Lawrence, dir. *Second Thoughts*. Universal Pictures, Associated Film Distribution, 1983. Film.

Underwood, Ron, dir. *Speechless*. Metro-Goldwyn-Mayer (MGM), 1994. Film.

Wacks, Jonathan, dir. *Powwow Highway*. Warner Bros., 1989. Film.

TOUR 4

Santa Funky

Start: The Cathedral Basilica of St. Francis de Assisi (131 Cathedral Place, Santa Fe, NM, 87501; 505-982-5619, cbsfa.org).

Distance: 2.2 miles (optional extension of 0.8 miles at the end of Canyon Road)

Time: 1 hour, 15 minutes

Highlights: The Cathedral Basilica of St. Francis de Assisi, Cathedral Park, Drury Plaza Hotel, Canyon Road, El Zaguán, PERA Building, Dragon Room, Barrio de Analco

Parking: Street parking along Cathedral Place or along Alameda Avenue.

Santa Fe probably wasn't your first thought for big action and laughs. It's an artistic destination known for fine eating, history, and culture. On screen, though, it's also a fine spot for comedians, action heroes, and really handsome aliens.

If you're winding up the previous tour, take Palace Avenue or East San Francisco Street toward the Cathedral Basilica of St. Francis de Assisi. The landmark is difficult to miss. It's a stone, Romanesque Revival titan amidst the shorter Pueblo-style buildings that surround it. The cathedral, despite the fact that it was never fully completed, is traditionally the tallest building in central Santa Fe. It was originally envisioned with 160-foot spiral extensions for the two towers, but they were never realized. There's even some uncertainty that the cathedral walls could have supported the added weight of the completed spirals, making the cathedral's unfinished edifice both a historical oddity and a bit of good fortune.

The unofficial "Heart of Santa Fe," the cathedral is associated with the legacy of Archbishop Jean-Baptiste Lamy. Born in France, Lamy trained as a Catholic priest before moving to the United States, where he was responsible for two parishes in Ohio. Then, in 1847, Lamy moved to Santa Fe, where his policies were effective but controversial. He reinstated tithing and fought with popular, established priests in the region. For his achievements, Lamy was named Bishop of the diocese. He also led construction of a massive cathedral in the center of Santa Fe. Inspired by the church in his native Auvergne, France, Lamy commissioned a structure to be made of stone with Roman-Byzantine stylings.

Work on the cathedral began in 1869. To build the Romanesque Revival structure, yellow limestone was quarried twenty miles south of Santa Fe by skilled masons who had been trained or raised in places like Italy and France. The cathedral was dedicated in 1886, although work on the structure continued for years.

Lamy may be best known as the protagonist of Willa Cather's 1927 novel *Death Comes for the Archbishop*. Cather made her mark in the early twentieth century with a series of novels about life on the frontier. She won the Pulitzer Prize for *One of Ours* in 1922. Lamy represented a slightly different style of frontier hero for Cather, but one that fit well into her aesthetic. She portrayed him as a dedicated public servant who traveled throughout New Mexico to do the work of the Church. The book is widely considered a classic but has never been adapted into film.

The cathedral makes a nice backdrop for a pivotal scene in the adaptation of the Broadway smash *RENT*. The play, loosely based on Puccini's classic *La Boheme*, premiered on Broadway in 1996. All told, it ran for more than a decade. Among the songs written for the play, "Santa Fe" explored the idea of moving to the City Different to escape the oppression of living in New York.

In the 2005 filmed adaptation of the hit musical, the tightknit group of friends at the heart of the story open up about their interests in moving to Santa Fe during a subway ride. The train becomes their stage as they dance away their aggravation with New York and express their fantasy for a sunnier future.

One of the characters in the film and play, Roger Davis, actually escapes to Santa Fe by car for a brief respite. Then, he changes his mind and returns to his friends in New York. The cathedral is clearly visible as Davis catches the bus home. He returns to New York just in time to stand by his girlfriend's side as her drug addiction threatens to claim her life.

RENT's Santa Fe interlude isn't a true representation of the city, since a rural bus stop in front of the cathedral doesn't actually exist. Instead, there is a renowned cultural site: The Institute of American Indian Arts (IAIA) Museum of Contemporary Native Arts (108 Cathedral Place, Santa Fe, NM 87501; 505-983-8900, iaia.edu). Specializing in Indigenous work created after 1962, the museum is tied to the IAIA, which has a college campus in the southern end of Santa Fe. Founded in 1962 by Cherokee artist and designer Lloyd Kiva New, the college specializes in the study of Native American art and heritage.

You can also spot the cathedral in the Ivan Reitman comedy *Twins* (1988). In a way, the film was an experiment about an experiment. Although Reitman had already established his comedic bona fides with the classic *Ghostbusters* (1984), putting action star Arnold Schwarzenegger in a part that depended more on punchlines than pushups was a risk. The studio was so concerned that they structured a special deal with Schwarzenegger, essentially cutting him in on the back end if he agreed to appear in the movie for a low upfront fee. Even stranger was the notion of pairing the hulking Austrian with the diminutive comedian Danny DeVito. The two play genetically engineered twins with the caveat that Schwarzenegger's character is the perfectly designed human, while DeVito's character was made of the leftovers.

The twins find each other and then go in search of their surrogate mother. Their journey takes them to Los Alamos and then to an artist's commune north of Santa Fe. (Parts of this scene shot at the Randall Davey Audubon Center & Sanctuary, 1800 Upper Canyon Road, Santa Fe, NM 87505; 505-983-4609 ext. 23, randalldavey.audubon.org.) Before meeting her, though, the brothers want to spruce up a little and go to downtown

Arnold Schwarzenegger and Danny DeVito with the Cathedral Basilica of St. Francis of Assisi behind them in *Twins* (1988). Courtesy of Universal Pictures.

Santa Fe to buy the sharpest suits they can find. Finely appointed, the brothers strut around in their new duds, with the Santa Fe cathedral making a cameo in the background.

The odd coupling worked, and the film announced Schwarzenegger as an unexpected comic voice. As a reward, he took home substantial back-end pay. His bet paid off in other ways, too. He went on to star in comedies like *Kindergarten Cop* (1990) and *True Lies* (1994). He even teamed up again with Danny DeVito for the ill-fated and uncomfortable comedy *Junior* (1994), in which Schwarzenegger's character gets pregnant.

With or without a new suit, you can go inside the cathedral on most days. The cathedral is still an active center for worship and schedules regular services. So please be conscientious. Note that the property can be toured for free but often closes in the early afternoon, so please check ahead if you plan to visit.

Although the cathedral dates back to the 1880s, the spot where it stands was home to the center of Catholic worship in the area as a far back as 1626. The original adobe-style church was destroyed during the Pueblo Revolt and replaced with La Parroquia, built during the mid-1700s. Lamy decided to replace that church but left it functional during construction. The new cathedral was erected around La Parroquia, which was slowly dismantled and moved out of the cathedral.

When you step in, you'll notice the neo-Corinthian columns near the double arches at the entry way. Up top, you can also spot a keystone arch with an engraving in Hebrew with the word for God. The inscription is probably meant to recognize the help of local Jewish merchants who proved instrumental to the construction of the cathedral. It's also hard to miss the stained glass window that was cast in France and installed in 1884. For a peek even further into the past, visit the Lady Chapel of the Cathedral Basilica of St. Francis of Assisi, the oldest part of the present-day cathedral, where La Conquistadora, Our Lady of Conquering Love, is housed. The religious icon is believed to be the oldest statue of the Virgin Mary in North America.

After you've had a look inside the chapel, exit to the right to explore the attached grounds. Three statues greet you in the park. Lamy, of course, is the most central. The bronze of him was dedicated in 1915. Nearby is an unpainted bronze of the patron saint of Santa Fe, St. Francis de Assisi. Here, he rests his hand upon a wolf that he has stopped from attacking Umbria in modern Italy. The final statue at the entrance belongs to St. Kateri Tekakwitha, the first Native American to be canonized. Sometimes called Lily of the Mohawks, Tekakwitha is the patron saint of the environment and Native peoples.

You'll find even more bronzes in the park just to your right. On the short path, note the labyrinth, which pays homage to a similar design in France. Once you've descended down the short ramp, you'll be in Cathedral Park, which commemorates Spanish pioneers with the Settlers Monument, a crowded bronze that features the likenesses of Spanish pioneers and Conquistador Don Diego de Vargas, who recaptured what is now New

Cathedral Park as it appeared in *National Treasure: Edge of History* (2022). Courtesy of Disney.

Mexico for Spain after the Pueblo Revolt of 1680. The park also features several plaques that explain this history in more detail.

The heroes of Disney+'s *National Treasure*: *Edge of History* (2022) take a break in the park to plan their next move in the search for a cache of historical artifacts moved from Mesoamerica and hidden somewhere in the United States. As they talk, the IAIA Museum of Contemporary Native Arts is visible in the background.

The ten-part television show was a short-lived reboot of the *National Treasure* (2004) and *National Treasure: Book of Secrets* (2007) blockbusters starring Nicolas Cage. The two films grabbed a cumulative 400 million dollars in domestic box office, making the franchise a natural choice for resurrection. The show reimagined the films as a season-long search for the lost treasure of the Aztecs, which had been moved and protected for centuries by a secret society. Lisette Olivera and Catherine Zeta-Jones starred.

Both Cathedral Park and the building to its north were once owned by the Archdiocese of Santa Fe and were used for healthcare. Archbishop

Lamy invited the Sisters of Charity to New Mexico and then sold the plot that is now Cathedral Park to them so they could open the St. Vincent Sanatorium at the same location in 1883.

The first building was destroyed in a fire in 1896 but was soon rebuilt on the same site. Eventually, the Sisters of Charity needed more room and asked noted architect John Gaw Meem to design a larger facility. Construction was completed in the 1950s and the building was used as a hospital until 1977. Afterward, the State of New Mexico took possession of the building and housed the Department of Cultural Affairs and the New Mexico State Film Office in the building. It also made for a convenient location for filming and for an alien god to convalesce.

Although it shot largely at what was then known as the Ford Ranch, a Western backlot near Galisteo, the fourth offering from the Marvel Cinematic Universe, *Thor*, made a brief detour to the old sanatorium. The film follows the exploits of the Norse god Thor who is banished to earth by his all-powerful father, Odin. After landing, Thor gets hit by an off-road vehicle called a Pinzgauer. Natalie Portman, playing Jane Foster, brings him to a hospital to convalesce. The interior of the hospital is, in fact, now the Drury Plaza Hotel. It doesn't take long for Thor to escape his confinement in the hospital bed, but he runs right back into the Pinzgauer in the hospital parking lot.

Directed by Kenneth Branagh and starring Chris Hemsworth as the fabled hero, *Thor* (2011) proved an international blockbuster grossing nearly 450 million dollars. It also laid the story groundwork for one of the highest-grossing films of all time, Marvel Studios' *The Avengers,* which shot largely in Albuquerque at Q Studios. Hemsworth reprised his role as Thor in that film and succeeding hit films in what has become the most valuable franchise in moviemaking history.

The present-day Drury Plaza Hotel was purchased in 2007 and renovated into luxury accommodations. It's a good option for staying in the area and frequently used by productions in Santa Fe.

From the Drury Plaza, walk up to Paseo de Peralta and make a right, then turn left on Canyon Road. You've possibly already heard of Santa Fe's most famous street, a wall-to-wall assembly of art galleries in a uniquely Santa Fe milieu. This tour will continue back down Paseo de Peralta, so walk down Canyon Road as much as you want and then turn around and retrace your path. You can also walk back along Alameda, if you'd like to cross the bridge past the Teahouse at East Palace Avenue.

Now the center of Santa Fe's vibrant gallery scene, Canyon Road has ancient roots. Once called Camino de Cañon, the path ran between Native American pueblos and later connected Spanish Santa Fe to the descendants of those communities. It's likely that the early trail followed the Santa Fe River, headed through the mountains and made its way to Pecos Pueblo, then an important center of trade. The road also became a thoroughfare for Spanish and Mexican soldiers hauling lumber out of the nearby Sangre de Cristo Mountains.

During the eighteenth century, a rural community sprang up along the road to take advantage of local water sources. Many of the homes built later during the Mexican period between 1821 and 1848 boast hallmark thick adobe walls, some of which are still visible around the area.

In the 1920s and 1930s, artists settled the corridor constructing small residences in the formerly agrarian plots. The first gallery in the area opened in the mid-1930s, prefiguring a trend that would explode several decades later. By the 1960s, Canyon Road found its modern form as a densely populated gallery space.

Although it's a year-round destination for art collectors, Canyon Road comes to life most on Christmas Eve when gallerists line the street with campfires and glowing luminarias, or farolitos. Many of these galleries stay open late to hand out cider, wine, and hot chocolate to families who are out on a stroll through the area. Canyon Road's festivities make a backdrop for scenes in the comedy *An Ideal Home* (2018), but more on that film later.

El Zaguán as it appeared in *News of the World* (2020). Courtesy of Universal Pictures.

Continue up Canyon Road to the Historic Santa Fe Foundation's El Zaguán adobe. The building is mostly a relic of the Santa Fe Trail period. Trader James L. Johnson, who made his fortune as a wholesaler, but who also held other interests in mining and banking, purchased the Canyon Road farmhouse in 1854 and soon began to expand it. After buying the neighboring parcels, he transformed the small farmhouse into a twenty-four-room estate. The Johnsons also added a garden, which they filled with imported and exotic plants. Johnson's wife, Maria Jesus, attended to the plants. The garden was later named in honor of a famed guest who stayed at the house, archaeologist Adolph Bandelier. (For more on Bandelier, check out the North of Santa Fe and Outdoor Adventure on page 97.)

After the Johnsons lost their fortune, they sold El Zaguán to the Catrons, who made their money in the Santa Fe Ring. The estate was passed along to several owners, including descendants of the Johnson family, before the Historic Santa Fe Foundation took possession of it. They carefully preserved the building and garden. Now, Historic Santa Fe uses it for art exhibits, residencies, and tours.

El Zaguán made an excellent endpoint for Tom Hanks in the closing minutes of *News of the World*. Here, a weary Hanks, as Jefferson Kyle Kidd, arrives home. To make the old building look even more period-appropriate, set decorators covered Canyon Road with dirt.


```
EXT. SAN ANTONIO SIDE STREET—DAY
Kidd turns off into a handsome side street.
Approaches an elegant Spanish style house.
Wrought iron railings.
Kidd stops. Looks up at it.

                                        CUT TO:

EXT. BETANCOURT HOUSE—DAY
Kidd peers through a window.
An empty hallway.
He runs his hand behind a rock . . . Finds a key.
Inserts it into the lock.

                                        CUT TO:

INT. BETANCOURT HOUSE—DAY
Kidd moves through the silent house.
Shutters closed.
Walls bare.
He goes up the stairs . . .
```

(From the script for *News of the World* written by Paul Greengrass and Luke Davies and based on the novel of the same name by Paulette Jiles)

Call Time: Getting Involved in the Industry

There are thousands of film workers in New Mexico, a significant number when compared to the state's overall population of just two million. We aren't, in other words, all that hard to find. If you're interested in getting into the business or getting connected to it, here are some places to start:

For local film festivals, try the Santa Fe International Film Festival (santafe.film). Formerly known as the Santa Fe Independent Film Festival, this event usually draws local talent and hosts a series of panels and screenings of films plucked from major festivals around the world. Down south, the Albuquerque Film and Music Experience (afmxnm.com) in the Duke City also offers some valuable programming. Both events are usually in the fall.

Almost all of the major educational institutions in the state have some kind of film curriculum, but Albuquerque's Central New Mexico

From El Zaguán, you can finish the walk up Canyon Road. If your budget allows, several of Santa Fe's best-known restaurants are about a block away. No restaurant is more synonymous with fine dining in Santa Fe than Geronimo (724 Canyon Road, Santa Fe, NM, 87501; 505-982-1500, geronimorestaurant.com). Their "global eclectic" cuisine is a magnet for Santa Fe's well-to-do. Geronimo also has the distinction of being housed in a historic property with roots dating back to the mid-eighteenth century. Preservationists purchased and restored the home piecemeal in the 1930s.

On the opposite side of Canyon Road, The Compound Restaurant (653 Canyon Road, Santa Fe, NM, 87501; 505-982-4353, compoundrestaurant.com) is award-winning chef Mark Kiffin's enduring Santa Fe classic. For tapas and live music, El Farol (808 Canyon Road, Santa Fe, NM, 87501; 505-983-9912, elfarolsantafe.com) is an excellent choice.

There are a number of return routes to the Cathedral Basilica from the end of the commercial stretch of Canyon Road. You can cross at the bridge past the Teahouse, or you can continue to the end of Canyon Road until it crosses Alameda. Otherwise, you can turn around and retrace your steps to Paseo de Peralta and make a left.

If you've eaten on Canyon Road, it might be time for dessert and a detour to Kakawa for some chocolate. Hang a right on Paseo de Peralta and go for about two blocks before you spot the small chocolate shop on your right-hand side. Inside, the walls feature framed photos of celebrities for a reason. Kakawa serves up distinctive hot drinking chocolate that it calls elixirs. The confections are influenced by traditional Mesoamerican drinking chocolates, some of which have historic ties to New Mexico. Vessels with traces of ancient similar concoctions were recently uncovered in Room 28 at Chaco Culture National Park, once the center of the Ancestral Puebloan world.

After satisfying your sweet tooth, cross the street to explore two more art galleries. The Gerald Peters Gallery and Gerald Peters Contemporary Gallery (1005 and 1011 Paseo de Peralta, Santa Fe, NM 87501; gpgallery.com) have substantive collections of Western, classic, and modern art in multiple mediums as well as constantly changing exhibitions.

Continue down Paseo de Peralta away from Canyon Road. Up ahead on your right, fronted by a large state parking lot, you'll see the PERA Building. Part of the capitol complex, the building's name is an acronym for Public Employees Retirement Association, although that organization has since moved to another location while other state offices have moved in to the PERA Building.

The building's colonnade, staircase, and high portico make it an excellent destination for scenes involving government entities. You can spot the building in *Waco: The Aftermath*. This

Community College (cnm.edu) offers a particularly strong program with specialized training for skilled gigs in the industry. In addition to associates degrees, the college also has a certificate for film crew training.

For locals interested in building their careers from the ground floor, the New Mexico film office offers occasional production assistant training. These courses run over several days and provide the lexicon and etiquette you'll need for the traditional entry-level production jobs. Please keep an eye on nmfilm.com for program dates.

If you're already into the industry and just need a little guidance for your shoot, try the film office for that as well. They can help with permitting and the state's incentive program.

You can also take a more organic approach. Many of the restaurants, hotels, and shops in this book are popular with people in the film industry. Often they're easy to spot, thanks to gifted t-shirts for crew members that spell out the projects they worked on.

sequel to the *Waco* miniseries moved the focus to the trial that proceeded the invasion of Koresh's compound and placed several scenes in central Santa Fe, including a pre-trial sequence at the PERA Building.

The author of this book in your hands made an appearance as background talent for a similar scene in *Outlaw Prophet*, but despite his convincing portrayal of "man at courthouse," the scene was later cut from the final film.

From the PERA Building, cross the parking lot and the street toward the state capitol at the corner of Old Santa Fe Trail (490 Old Santa Fe Trail, Santa Fe, NM 87501; 505-986-4589, nmlegis.gov/visitors). Often called the Roundhouse, the New Mexico State Capitol is one of the more unique state edifices in the country. The circular design pays homage to the traditional community kivas of the Pueblos, while the footprint is in the shape of the Zia Sun. Inside, the walls of the Roundhouse are decorated with some six hundred pieces from the Capitol Art Collection. Established in 1992, the collection was created by legislative act with the intent to showcase work from New Mexican artists. Highlights from the permanent and temporary collections are visible as you walk around the capitol.

The capitol is open for guided and self-guided tours during regular work hours. There's also a downloadable guide available on their website.*

Look out for the capitol's exterior to appear in the mixed family comedy, *An Ideal Home*. There aren't many films that bask in the milieu of Santa Fe as much as *An Ideal Home*. The comedy delves into Southwestern cooking, style, and living. In the film, British comedian Steve Coogan plays a famed food personality who spends his days throwing lavish parties and demonstrating regional cooking techniques on his television show. Coogan's character, Erasmus Brumble, has a contentious but affectionate relationship with his producer and lover, who is played by Paul Rudd. Their perfect partnership is interrupted by the arrival of Brumble's grandson, whose favorite meal is the Crunchwrap at Taco Bell. Ultimately, the three become a tempestuous but loving family.

The story had roots in Fleming's real-life experience co-raising his longtime partner's son. Although he never viewed the film as a polemic, he

* nmlegis.gov/Publications/Visitors/BrochureEnglish.pdf

was interested in exploring the idea of same-sex couple's imperfect parenting, that could be successful if not conventional or "ideal."

An Ideal Home also shot at the nearby Dragon Room—a funky, woodsy bar attached to The Pink Adobe restaurant (406 Old Santa Fe Trail Santa Fe, NM 87501; 505-983-2979, thepinkadobe.com). Walk down Old Santa Fe Trail away from Paseo de Peralta to find it. Founded in 1944, The Pink Adobe is something of a New Mexico classic; a plaque on the side of the restaurants claims it once hosted presidents and other dignitaries. The Dragon Room is slightly less refined, featuring plenty of winged lizard decor and mixed drinks.

From the Dragon Room, make a left on Old Santa Fe Trail and head to East De Vargas. On your right, you'll spot the adobe San Miguel Mission church, located in the Barrio de Analco, a national historic district of Santa Fe. Billed as the oldest church in the United States, the structure dates back to around 1610, and some of the interior walls still include adobe from that time period. Like other missions in New Mexico, the church was designed to minister the Christian faith to the Indigenous populations. San Miguel, in particular, was built to proselytize Indigenous Tlaxcalans from Mexico who were forcibly relocated to Santa Fe to provide labor. Many of these Tlaxcalans lived in the surrounding Barrio de Analco.

The church was nearly destroyed during the Pueblo Revolt of 1680. Several decades later, the Spanish rebuilt the church to accommodate their soldiers. The newly rebuilt church was finished in 1710, nearly one hundred years after its predecessor.

Mario Lopez's Christmas celebration, *Holiday in Santa Fe* (2021), shot at San Miguel. A classic Hallmark-style family-get-together flick, the film was originally slated to shoot elsewhere, but after Lopez and the crew scouted Santa Fe, they insisted that the film be reworked to shoot in the City Different. The resulting heart-warmer used much of central Santa Fe.

Have a look inside the church and then cross East De Vargas for another peek into the past. The "Oldest House in Santa Fe" has a tenuous claim to its ancient roots. Archaeologist Adolph Bandelier believed the foundations of the building went all the way back to around AD 1250. Contemporary research, though, dates parts of the building to the mid-1700s. The building and the small neighborhood around it housed the Tlaxcalans and other forced laborers from Mexico. The house is now a small museum with an attached gift shop.

You can wrap up the tour here, or head back to the plaza to link up with the other tours. To get there, continue down Old Santa Fe Trail past Alameda and past Water Street.

From here, a car will be useful for the additional tours. Bonus points if you have a 1960 Chevrolet Corvette.

Selected Filmography

Branagh, Kenneth, dir. *Thor*. Marvel Studios, 2011. Film.

Columbus, Chris, dir. *RENT*. Columbia Pictures, 2005. Film.

Fleming, Andrew. *An Ideal Home*. Remstar Studios, 2018. Film.

Greengrass, Paul, dir. *News of the World*. Universal Pictures, 2020. Film.

Hahn, Jody Margolin, dir. *Holiday in Santa Fe*. Lifetime Television, 2021. Television.

Reitman, Ivan, dir. *Twins*. Universal Pictures, 1988. Film.

Wibberley, Cormac and Marianne, creators. *National Treasure: Edge of History*. Disney+, 2023. Television.

Part II

Driving Tours

TOUR 5

Greater Santa Fe

Thanks to its signature design and ancient streets, downtown Santa Fe is beautiful, but it's not right for many productions that seek to replicate other parts of the United States or the world. Most of these publicly viewable locations are easy drives from the plaza. If you're determined to go by human power, some can be reached on the Rail Trail, a 15-mile path that parallels the railroad track used historically by the Atchison, Topeka and Santa Fe Railway. More recently, some segments of the tracks have been reclaimed by the New Mexico Rail Runner.

The easiest way to reach these locations, though, is to drive down Cerrillos Road, Santa Fe's commercial corridor that was once part of historic Route 66. Until 1937, the route worked its way south to Albuquerque and included a precipitous drop at La Bajada hill before a more gradual trail was built near present-day I-25. Today, Cerrillos Road goes to southern Santa Fe and ultimately to Tijeras near Albuquerque. The road is also known as New Mexico State Road 14, or the Turquoise Trail National Scenic Byway. (For more on some of the attractions on the byway, check out the South of Santa Fe Driving Tour on page 84.) You can pick up Cerrillos Road off Paseo de Peralta and head south away from the plaza.

On your left, you'll spot The Sage Hotel just before the turn to Cerrillos. This relatively inexpensive lodge was used in the first episode of the second season of *Waco*. There's a bar with live music on premise if you'd like to stop. Otherwise, continue down Cerrillos.

Before crossing Saint Francis, just past the Whole Foods on the left, be on the lookout for Early Street on the same side. You can turn there to get a quick look at the Fraternal Order of Eagles (FOE) #2811 (833 Early Street, Santa Fe, NM 85705; 505-983-7171, foe.com), a site used in the Netflix action thriller *Trigger Warning* (2024) and a meeting space for the nonprofit organization of the same name. *Trigger Warning* stars Jessica Alba as a veteran who returns home to inherit the family bar, with the FOE playing the part. The building itself is accessible only to members unless public events are posted. Afterward, the easiest thing to do is make a left on Calle Grillo and then another left to Don Diego Avenue, which will return you to Cerrillos Road.

Just off Cerrillos Road is the Santa Fe Indian School (1501 Cerrillos Road, Santa Fe, NM 87502; 505-989-6300, sfis.k12.nm.us), one of Santa Fe's oldest and most important cultural institutions. It can be easy to miss unless you're paying attention. Founded in 1890 with the express purpose of assimilating Native American children into white society, the former boarding school is now owned and operated by the nineteen Pueblos of New Mexico.

Still a functioning school, SFIS featured in the sports comedy *Rez Ball* (2024), directed by Sydney Freeland and written by Sterlin Harjo. Freeland and Harjo previously worked together on the show *Reservation Dogs* (2021), which pioneered television as the first television serial to be wholly written and directed by Indigenous talent. *Rez Ball* had another major talent behind the lens as well: basketball star LeBron James, who produced it via his company SpringHill. On screen, you can look out for New Mexican Amber Midthunder, as Dezbah Weaver, a petulant friend of the team's star player.

The film is based on the book *Canyon Dreams: A Basketball Season on the Navajo Nation* written by *New York Times* journalist Michael Powell, which tells the story of a high school team in Chinle, Arizona. The film relocates the story to the fictional Chuska, New Mexico, where the Chuska Warriors are vying for the state championship but must overcome the loss of their star player in the process.

In addition to work in Santa Fe, the film shot on the Navajo Nation in New Mexico. Called Dinétah by its people, the Navajo Nation is the largest Native American reservation in the United States, encompassing a geographical swath larger than the state of Maryland. Famously, the Navajo

Nation is home to Monument Valley, the red stone towers made iconic by filmmakers like John Ford. Check out the film history introduction on page xx for more details on nearby Gallup, where many filmmakers stayed on the way to Monument Valley.

The Santa Fe Indian School is open to the public on occasion. Keep an eye out for performances held in their theater. Otherwise, the school can only be viewed in passing.

If thinking about all this exercise has made you hungry, you're near some great spots for a bite. Not as frequented by tourists as the plaza, central Santa Fe has a number of charming eateries and coffee spots when it's time for a break. Make a left on 2nd Street off Cerrillos, and straight ahead you'll see Back Road Pizza (1807 2nd St. #1, Santa Fe, NM, 87505; 505-955-9055, backroadpizza.com), which is excellent for a break with the family. You can also make a left on Lena Street to visit the hip Lena Street Lofts. There you'll find the Iconik Coffee Roasters flagship store (1600 Lena Street Suite A2, Santa Fe, NM 87505; 505-428-0996, iconikcoffee.com), a good spot to refuel and plan your next move. Just down the road, you'll spot The Bread Shop (1703 Lena Street, Santa Fe, NM 87505; 505-230-8421, breadshopsf.com). In addition to fresh baked goods, you can also find fresh fashion and pottery in the area. You can head back to Cerrillos after your break and hang a left.

New Mexican Filmmakers of Note

Mae Marsh (silent film actor): Born in Madrid, New Mexico, Marsh joined her sister, Marguerite, in Los Angeles, where the two pursued acting from childhood. Beginning her career as a "freckle-faced girl," Marsh transformed into one of director D.W. Griffith's preferred stars and played a pivotal role in his epochal *Birth of a Nation*. After films moved to sound, Marsh found frequent work in supporting roles.

Drew Goddard (screenwriter): Raised in Los Alamos, Goddard wrote for television shows including *Alias* (2001–2006) and *Buffy the Vampire Slayer* (1997–2003). He is best known for adapting Andy Weir's novel *The Martian* (2011) into a film of the same name in 2015. Goddard credited the scientists he grew up around in Los Alamos for inspiring the positivity and ingenuity prevalent among the astronaut heroes in the film.

Mae Marsh on the cover of *Photoplay* magazine, September 1917. Wikimedia Commons.

Amber Midthunder (actor): The Midthunders are New Mexico film royalty. Amber's father, David, is a stunt technician and actor. Her mother, Angelique, runs a casting agency with an impressive array of credits on projects like FX's *Reservations Dogs*. For her part, Amber has shined in a number of breakout roles, notably in the FX sci-fi mind-bender *Legion* (2017-2019), *Roswell, New Mexico*, and the *Predator* (1987) franchise reboot *Prey* (2022).

Neil Patrick Harris (actor): The Albuquerque native achieved international fame as a child star in the show *Doogie Howser, M.D.* (1989–1993) and then refashioned his career as an adult in *How I Met Your Mother* (2005–2014).

Continue down Cerrillos to the Cottonwood Court Motel (1742 Cerrillos Rd, Santa Fe, NM 87505; 505-982-5571) on your left. Actor and director Clint Eastwood made a brief stop here alongside an unusual companion—an orangutan named Clyde. Eastwood played Philo Beddoe, a trucker and bare-knuckled fighter punching his way across the West in search of a woman he met in a bar who disappeared not long after he fell for her. His travels take him to Santa Fe and the Cottonwood Court Motel, where he gets dropped off after hitchhiking.

The greater journey, though, was for Eastwood himself, who had spent the last decade establishing himself as a Western and action star in films like *Dirty Harry* (1971) and *The Outlaw Josey Wales* (1976). That reputation had been cemented partially on the strength of his previous work in New Mexico. Following, his success in Sergio Leone's *Man with No Name* (1964–1966) trilogy, Eastwood produced *Hang 'Em High* (1968), his first Western filmed in the United States. *Hang 'Em High* launched Eastwood's production company Malpaso and announced him as more than a silent, brooding character actor.

Amazingly, Eastwood returned to New Mexico decades later to direct and star in *The Mule* (2018), which shot in Las Cruces, and *Cry Macho* (2021), primarily filmed in Albuquerque. Somehow, Eastwood has managed to star in action films at more than eighty years of age, but he only acted along aside a primate twice: in *Every Which Way but Loose* (1978), and its sequel, *Any Which Way You Can* (1980). You can continue south down Cerrillos away from the plaza.

A few blocks from the Cottonwood Court Motel, you'll spot the El Rey Court (1862 Cerrillos Road, Santa Fe, NM 87505; 505-982-1931, elreycourt.com). Like the Cottonwood, this historic hotel has a filmic tie to a legend.

Perhaps no author is as closely identified with New Mexico as mystery writer Tony Hillerman, who transformed his experiences as a journalist traveling the Southwest into a best-selling series of novels about fictional Navajo detectives Jim Chee and Joe Leaphorn. The books attracted the attention of Robert Redford, who purchased the rights to some of the books and produced several films for PBS. Wes Studi and Adam Beach starred in the first adaptation, *Skinwalkers: The Mysteries* (2002). Chris Eyre, famed for the indie darling *Smoke Signals* (1998), directed the initial three episodes of the miniseries. A second film, *A Thief of Time* (2003) followed. A third adaptation, directed by Jan Egleson, premiered the same year.

Redford retained the rights to Hillerman's writing and approached George R. R. Martin to help revive the project years later. According to his blog, Martin met Hillerman upon moving to New Mexico in 1979. Martin was immediately impressed with both Hillerman's personality and his novels. Martin, still riding high on the success of *Game of Thrones*, made a natural partner. They brought on writer Graham Roland and adapted Hillerman's *Listening Women* and *People of Darkness* into a ten-part television series for AMC called *Dark Winds* (2022). (The series is not to be confused with a 1991 Hillerman adaptation named *Dark Wind*. This take on Hillerman starred Lou Diamond Phillips as Jim Chee and Fred Ward as Joe Leaphorn. Errol Morris, who would later win an Academy Award for his documentary *The Fog of War* (2003), directed.)

Chris Eyre reprised his role behind the camera for the 2022 rendition, but actors Zahn McClarnon and Kiowa Gordon took on the central characters. The show ran for one season and was quickly renewed for a second and then a third. It shot around Española and Santa Fe, including at El Rey, among Santa Fe's trendiest motels.

Part of the Route 66 boom that enveloped the Southwest, El Rey Court was once among a number of inexpensive but dependable places to crash along the drive from the Midwest to California. (For more on Route 66, check out the Road Trip tour on page 41.) Built in 1936, El Rey had fallen into some disrepair until a couple from California joined forces with investors from Texas to remodel it after their purchase in 2016. The group had an eye toward making it a hip, off-downtown destination for drinking and lounging. The newly improved El Rey includes a bar called La Reina and an expanded pool, and some rooms that have been modernized.

After checking out the hotel, continue down Cerrillos, make a left on Saint Michael's Drive, and then make an immediate right onto the midtown campus, which might be closed and secured, so take note. Among the more integral locations to the Santa Fe film scene, the campus formerly known as the Santa Fe University of Art and Design is home to both a film studio and a theater used for independent films called The Screen. Initially funded by the actor Greer Garson, the studios that would soon bear her name eventually incorporated three stages. Not as large and versatile as the Q Studios in Albuquerque, or the Santa Fe Studios, Garson has still carved a useful space in the New Mexico production world. The studio has hosted a long line of films and television shows that have used not only its stage space but also the assortment of nearby empty buildings currently not in use because the university closed in 2018. Redevelopment plans are ongoing. Among other shows, Garson has been home base for *Young Guns 2* (1990), *Wyatt Earp* (1994), the HBO televised play *The Sunset Limited* (2011), and *Outer Range* (2022). At one point, the studio got so busy that productions were routinely bumping into each other. Jessica Dias, a producer on *Longmire*, which also used the studio, told the *Santa Fe Reporter*, "We've had problems with extras and people showing up for casting sessions here when they were trying to get to *Manhattan*, and we've had actors dropped off on the wrong set." The two productions should have been impossible to confuse.

While *Longmire* used Garson and greater Santa Fe to stage a rendition of contemporary Wyoming, *Manhattan* (2014–2015) recreated the most secretive moments of the Second World War. In its way, the show was all about secrets. Sam Shaw conceived of the pilot as an investigation into the toll of secrets on a community of scientists and their family lives. Initially, he wrote the show as a sample, intended to demonstrate his talent and not to be produced. The established director Tommy Schlamme, though, read the teleplay and saw the potential.

He and the rest of the crew, likewise, saw the potential of a cluster of World War II–era army barracks near the Garson Studios. The buildings made great starting blocks for constructing an historically accurate representation of the Manhattan Project. The production repainted the exteriors of the aged buildings and filled them with period-appropriate office equipment, including typewriters and wire recorders. The transportation department also sourced wartime vehicles, some of which proved exceedingly difficult to drive with their rudimentary steering and gear shifts. When complete, the barracks were transformed into labs, dormitories, a school, a PX and a theater. The complex was later damaged in a fire and then razed by the city, potentially making way for additional development in the area.

The show also recreated their own version of "the gadget," or a model of the atomic bomb itself. This life-size contraption was taken to Bonanza Creek Ranch and set atop a tower, where the pivotal scenes of the final episodes of the show unfolded. Despite rave critical reviews, the show's network, WGN America, changed their content strategy and dropped the show. For more on Bonanza Creek Ranch, check out the South of Santa Fe driving tour.

Garson Studios is not available to the public, but The Screen is currently under renovation by the owner of Sky Cinemas and may soon reopen as part of an expanded multiplex.

After driving past or near Garson, you can return to Cerrillos and head left. There's a gem of local cuisine and an unexpected filming location in the shopping center. Jambo Café (2010 Cerrillos Road, Santa Fe, NM

87505; 505-473-1269, jambocafe.net) serves arguably the best Jamaican/Caribbean food in the state.

One of the more unique television shows made in the state, *The Curse* (2023), attempted to blend narrative entertainment with a reality styling. At the helm, and in front of the camera, Nathan Fielder brought the trademark candid awkwardness that he used to establish his reputation in projects like *Nathan for You* (2013) and *The Rehearsal* (2022–2025). In the latter, he blurred the lines between reality and performance art to such a degree it became difficult to disentangle acting from real-life events.

Fielder's work impressed indie film director Benny Safdie, one of the brotherly duo behind the films *Good Times* (2017) and *Uncut Gems* (2019). Safdie sought out Fielder and the two discussed an exchange Fielder once had with a panhandler who placed a curse on him. The incident would make for the spine of a television show. They were also fascinated with reality television.

The two auteurs created a show about a couple, Fielder and Emma Stone as Asher and Whitney Siegel, attempting to launch an HGTV-style reality series. Their plan is to set up an eco-friendly real estate company and also to make community investments throughout Española. From the beginning, though, it's apparent that their good intentions may not be genuine and their methodology may not be moral. After a television interview gone awry, Fielder's character attempts to steal information from a casino to distract from the potential negative press and his robbery turns into a debacle reminiscent of Fielder's work in reality TV in both pacing and location.

"We wanted it to be as realistic as possible. We only wanted to cast people from the neighborhood. We wanted the real place to be in the show with us, so there would be a dialogue between us," Safdie told *The Hollywood Reporter*. To capture that authenticity, the show cast real-life people to populate their version of Española and then complemented them with some actual locations.

Look for Jambo Café to make an appearance in the second episode during a pivotal business lunch in which Fielder and Stone's character, Whitney Siegel, have an awkward exchange with a local artist. Siegel believes that the artist is key to her plans to create a real estate and media empire. She spends much of the show chasing her relationship with this artist, played by Nizhonniya Austin, who came up as a production assistant on New Mexico films and then broke through in this role. Stop by the restaurant before heading straight down Cerrillos to the next location.

On the right at 2841 Cerrillos stands the site of what was once Santa Fe's only strip club, a joint called Cheeks. Shuttered in 2021, the bar made an appearance in *Thor* as a local watering hole where the exiled titular god engages with a human tradition he enjoys: drinking. He and Dr. Erik Selvig, played by the eponymous Stellan Skarsgård, knock back boilermakers on their way to bonding. Skarsgård reprised his role in several more Marvel Cinematic Universe films. There's no particular reason to stop at this strip mall, so you can continue on down to a larger shopping center.

The Santa Fe Place Mall (4250 Cerrillos Road, Santa Fe NM, 87507) is home to chain and big box stores. Perhaps it's not the stuff of souvenir shopping, but if you want to stop by, the mall was used for the pivotal ending of *Odd Thomas*. Otherwise, make a left on Rodeo Road for the next stop.

Santa Fe's Western heart is actually here on the southern end of town. The Rodeo de Santa Fe is a local institution founded in 1949. The rodeo hosts seasonal barrel racing, 4-H events and, of course, their premier rodeo in June. The Netflix film *Walk. Ride. Rodeo.* (2019) told the true story of Amberley Snyder, a championship barrel racer from Utah who lost the use of her legs after a car accident. Through physical therapy, Snyder didn't regain full mobility but was able to work her way back to riding and then the rodeo, hence the film's title. The movie shot mostly in Santa Fe, with a number of scenes at the rodeo. Check their website for the schedule before going. (3237 West Rodeo Road, Santa Fe, NM 87507; 505-471-4300, rodeodesantafe.org).

From here, you can head down to the South of Santa Fe road-trip tour. To do that, make a right out of the rodeo and a left on New Mexico State Road 14, which heads to the town of Cerrillos. To return to the plaza, take New Mexico State Road 14 to I-25 North.

Or, you can return to the plaza by making a left on Rodeo Road and work your way to Old Pecos Trail. This road, which becomes Old Santa Fe Trail closer to the plaza, is a historical remnant of ancient Native American paths and the Santa Fe Trail. Not named idly, the trail used to make its way to the historic village of Pecos, where you can now find Pecos National Historical Park (1 Peach Drive, Pecos NM 87552; 505-757-7241, nps.gov/peco/), an eighteenth-century mission and attached pueblo. Nearby, the Pecos River and the Monastery Lake are both popular filming locations and can be spotted in *Longmire, True Grit,* and others.

If you choose not to head north toward Pecos, go down Old Pecos Trail and keep an eye out for the Pecos Trail Inn, another decades-old remnant of America's cross-country heyday. The hotel claims to have once hosted John Wayne (2239 Old Pecos Trail, Santa Fe, New Mexico, 87505; 505-982-1943, thepecostrailinn.com). *Dark Winds* shot at this hotel as well. Continue on Old Pecos to Camino Lejo and make a right, following the signs to Museum Hill.

Santa Fe's primary concentration of museums outside of the plaza, Museum Hill is one-stop shopping for premier cultural institutions. Here you'll find the New Mexico Laboratory of Anthropology library, founded in 1930 and now part of the Museum of Indian Arts and Culture (710 Camino Lejo, Santa Fe, NM 87505; 505-476-1269, indianartsandculture.org).The Wheelwright Museum of the American Indian (704 Camino Lejo, Santa Fe, NM 87505; 505-982-4636, wheelwright.org) was founded in 1937 with the express purpose of preserving Navajo decorative artifacts. The Museum of International Folk Art (706 Camino Lejo, Santa Fe, New Mexico 87505; 505-476-1204, internationalfolkart.org), is sneakily among the most popular museums in the city thanks to its premier collection of figurines. And the Spanish Colonial Arts Society (750 Camino Lejo, Santa Fe, NM 87505;

spanishcolonial.org). Not surprisingly, the enclave of museums made a nice backdrop for an episode of *Antique Road Show* that aired in 2023. An anchor of programming for PBS, *Antique Road Show* first premiered in the United Kingdom in 1979 and was adapted for American audiences in 1997.

From Museum Hill, you can drive back to Old Pecos Trail and make a right to return to the plaza. Alternatively, you can retrace your route along Old Pecos Trail to the I-25 and the next driving tour.

Selected Filmography

Allyn, Conor, dir. *Walk. Ride. Rodeo*. Netflix, 2019. Film.

Fargo, James, dir. *Every Which Way But Loose*. Warner Bros, 1978. Film.

Fielder, Nathan, and Benny Safdie, creators. *The Curse*. Showtime, 2023. TV series.

Freeland, Sydney, dir. *Rez Ball*. Netflix, 2024. Film.

Roland, Graham, creator. *Dark Winds*. AMC, 2022. TV series.

Shaw, Sam, creator. *Manhattan*. WGN America, 2014–2015. TV series.

Sourya, Mouly, dir. *Trigger Warning*. Netflix, 2024. Film.

TOUR 6

South of Santa Fe

Despite Santa Fe's authentic historical character, most period films made near the city create their Western charm south of the plaza. No less than three Western film ranches and several historic mining communities are an easy drive from the plaza.

This drive can be done in segments or in one busy day and includes about two hours of driving time. I haven't timed it on horseback, but expect that ride to take at least a day.

From the plaza, take Old Santa Fe Trail to I-25 South and continue to the La Cienega exit. Hang right on La Cienega and stay with this winding road until it becomes Los Pinos. From New Mexico State Road 14, take the 599 crossover to West Frontage Road and then to Los Pinos off that road. You'll spot El Rancho Las Golondrinas (334 Los Pinos Road, Santa Fe, NM 87507; 505-471-2261, golondrinas.org), which can be easy to miss, so keep your eyes open.

Once, this historic ranch was a stop along the royal road, or the El Camino Real Tierra Adentro, which ran through New Spain from modern-day Mexico City to northern New Mexico. At the time, Las Golondrinas was a working ranch that was sometimes used as lodging for travelers. The ranch also became a trading post. Then, in the 1960s, ownership converted the property into a living history museum and preserved many of the traditional buildings on the site.

Not surprisingly, the ranch's collection of antique buildings makes an ideal location for period films, like Westerns, or even for mimicking exotic destinations like Old Mexico.

The ranch first appeared in the sequel to *Butch Cassidy and the Sundance Kid* (1969). This Paul Newman and Robert Redford classic reimagined the Western with a pop sensibility. Following it up was no easy task. The first

Actor and athlete Johnny Mack Brown featured in *Photoplay*, February 2, 1924. Wikimedia Commons.

film concludes with the outlaw heroes surrounded by the Bolivian army with little chance of survival. Following their further adventures would have been a liberal interpretation of both history and the film. Screenwriter William Goldman, who won an Academy Award for the first film, suggested that the sequel actually go back in time and introduce the outlaws before the apex of their careers.

Billy the Kid

New Mexico is home to countless artisans, the atomic age, entrepreneurs, and athletes, but its most famous citizen remains a teenage criminal who managed to get himself killed at the ripe old age of twenty-one.

Billy the Kid's true name, place of birth, and even his exact age all remain mysteries. Most scholars think that the Kid was born in New York around 1859, part of a surge of Irish immigrants who relocated to the city. In all likelihood, he then moved west with his family as a toddler, eventually settling in New Mexico. Going by Henry McCarty, Henry Antrim, or William H. Bonney, the Kid established his reputation as an outlaw while still a teenager by killing a bar braggart in Arizona after a short scuffle.

Just a few years later, already a known ruffian, the Kid found himself in the middle of a range war in Lincoln County. He allied with Englishman John Tunstall, fighting against James Dolan, Lawrence Murphy, and their supporters in the Santa Fe Ring. Bonney's skills as a fighter and cowhand made him a valuable asset for Tunstall. His improving abilities as an escape artist, though, made him into a legend.

Bonney made his first getaway early in his teens, but his final dash to freedom turned him into a romantic icon. In April 1881, only days away from execution for the assassination of Sheriff William Brady in Lincoln, Bonney was under lock and key at the Lincoln County Courthouse. The building served as a temporary holding cell for locally sentenced

The only confirmed photo of Billy the Kid. Courtesy of Fort Sumner. Wikimedia Commons.

criminals, the second story rigged with chains and cuffs.

Somehow Bonney secured both a pistol and the drop on one of his guards. He shot his way to freedom and then rode away, still wearing his handcuffs. Instead of absconding to Mexico, the Kid chose to stay in the United States, unwilling or unable to leave his adopted home and, perhaps, a woman.

Sticking around, Bonney turned himself into an easy-to-find target for Sheriff Pat Garrett, who tracked him down on the Maxwell Ranch and shot him in the back in the middle of the night.

Instead of disappearing in relative ignominy, the young outlaw transformed into a legend. He became the subject of newspaper articles, dime novels, and then motion pictures. Few fictional or historical characters have generated as much celluloid as the Kid. He's been the subject of roughly eighty films. In one film, he even dueled the undying in the appropriately named *Billy the Kid vs. Dracula* (1966). The Kid prevails by abandoning his six-shooter for a silver stake. In the long run, Dracula took the upper hand—Bram Stoker's creation is one of the few fictional or historical characters who has eclipsed the Kid's legacy on film.

A handful of these Billy the Kid films shot in New Mexico. Football star Johnny Mack Brown starred in Gore Vidal's rendition of the Kid's story made in Gallup. Emilio Estevez gave the part a shot while working near Santa Fe in Cerrillos. Dane Dehaan went under the hat as well, that rendition shooting in Rancho de las Golondrinas.

The historical Kid's legacy in Santa Fe pops up in a few places. Although it seems like a far cry from the lawlessness of Lincoln County, Bonney made an impression at the Palace of the Governors. He exchanged a series of letters with Territorial Governor Lew Wallace and even made a clandestine arrangement to turn state's witness.

Bonney agreed to provide an account of the murder of Huston J. Chapman. He saw the lawyer gunned down in cold blood in an exchange for being a stool pigeon. Bonney believed he would receive immunity. Ultimately, Bonney fulfilled his part of the bargain, but Wallace did not.

Awaiting trial, Bonney did time in Santa Fe. A placard at 208 W. San Francisco St., near Collected Works bookstore, indicates the spot where Bonney was held before he was transferred to Lincoln. Perhaps Wallace was too far away to hear Bonney's cries, but Bonney continued to write letters to the governor.

You can also catch up with the outlaw in the Las Vegas chapter. For the truly devout fan, though, a trip to Lincoln is the ultimate pilgrimage. And for the authoritative read on the Kid, Robert Utley's *Billy the Kid: A Short and Violent Life* remains the best work on the outlaw.

Although the first film made Robert Redford a star and cemented Paul Newman's legacy, neither of them returned for *Butch and Sundance: The Early Days*. Instead, Tom Berenger played a more youthful Butch Cassidy and William Katt stepped in as the Sundance Kid. The crew shot all over New Mexico and southern Colorado. (The 1969 film shot in southern Colorado as well, famously making use of the Durango and Silverton Railroad.) At Las Golondrinas, production constructed a mining office, which became a useful addition to the ranch's collection of genuine historic structures.

Elsewhere in the historic ranch, the variety of structures has enticed more than thirty productions to use the property in a multitude of genres from Western to slapstick to romantic comedy. You can reach the locations on a brief walk through the ranch. Or you can look out for the spots on the ranch's self-guided or docent-led tour.

Not far from the entrance to the ranch, several buildings were used in 2017's *The Kid* to replicate the Maxwell House in southern New Mexico where William Bonney, a.k.a. Billy the Kid, met his end at Pat Garrett's hand. Directed by actor Vincent D'Onofrio, *The Kid* took an unusual approach to the story of Billy the Kid, choosing to focus not on the teenage quickdraw himself, but rather on a boy who idolized him and eventually learned that Billy's allure was dangerous.

Moving farther into the ranch, look out for a small lake that appeared in the 1997 romantic comedy *Fools Rush In*. Salma Hayek took a float in the small body of water, fictionally placed in Mexico, not New Mexico. Apparently the scantily clad Hayek had trouble staying warm because the scene was staged in the dead of winter.

Walk around the lake and head toward one additional film location atop the hill to the Morada de Nuestra Señora de la Paz. The church appears in a parody of the 1980s television show *MacGyver* (1985). which starred Richard Dean Anderson as an agent for the fictional Phoenix Foundation. Anderson's character had a knack for getting himself in trouble and a talent for getting out of that trouble with contraptions assembled from any nearby resource. Comedian Will Forte's send-up of *MacGyver* first appeared as a

Saturday Night Live (1975–present) skit. MacGruber follows an ingenious covert operative who perhaps isn't quite as clever as he thinks he is. After the death of a friend, MacGruber retires to a monastery high in the mountains for spiritual healing. That monastery, of course, is the Morada de Nuestra Señora de la Paz.

To get there, you'll have to climb up the short hill after the creek crossing. This meeting house of the Penitentes, a fraternal order of Catholicism with roots in New Mexico in the eighteenth century, is actually a reproduction of a structure in Abiquíu, and it includes a chapel and a dining room.

After you've sauntered through the rest of the rancho, hop back in your car for the next stop on this route, perhaps the most iconic and frequented film location in the state. Turn left on Los Pinos Road and again on Entrada La Cienega. Then take I-25 south to the next exit, Bonanza Creek Road, and make a right and then a left. The gated entrance to the film ranch will be on your left-hand side. Some of the ranch is visible from the road, but to see the center of the faux Western town, you'll have to take a guided tour, which have been available in the past but are not currently.

Prior to its reinvention as a film ranch, or functional backlot for films, Bonanza Creek Ranch was a working cattle range and even the site of a short-lived gold rush. That changed in 1954 when the Anthony Mann–directed Western *The Man from Laramie* (1955) made plans to shoot on what was then called the Jarrett Ranch. Rumor has it that the production heard about the ranch through a friend of silent film star Mary Pickford. In any event, word got out that the ranch was an ideal location for Westerns, and a parade of films followed.

The Legend of the Lone Ranger not only used the ranch but constructed an expansive set. Their Western town, though, did not survive the weather. Later the European production *Lucky Luke* constructed their own period Western town nestled at the foot of three rounded hills in the heart of the ranch. The newly built backlot featured twenty-five structures, including a massive centerpiece saloon. The sets for *Lucky Luke* tolerated the wind and snow, making the ranch one of the few true backlots in all of New Mexico.

Jimmy Stewart and Alex Nicol at Tesuque in *The Man from Laramie*, © 1955 (renewed 1983) by Columbia Pictures Industries, Inc. All Rights Reserved. Courtesy of Columbia Pictures and the Paul Andrew Hutton Collection.

Much of the Western town will look familiar from films like *Silverado* (1986) or even Adam Sandler's *Ridiculous 6* (2015), but *Cowboys & Aliens* in particular featured a number of shots at the large, two-story saloon in the center of the town. Another landmark, the freestanding church at the end of the town, had a prominent role in the beginning of the Netflix Western *The Harder They Fall* (2021). Directed by musician Jeymes Samuel, a.k.a. The Bullitts, the film attempts to bring musical syncopation and modern beats to a class Western formula.

The Eastern side of the ranch has its own landmarks and began with construction for Terence Hill's Christmas film, *Botte di Natale* (1994). The crew built a two-story home by a small pond on the ranch. Like the main Western town, the pond house became a frequent set for films and appeared in *Perpetual Grace, LTD*, among others. Nearby, other productions constructed a series of World War II barracks, a large barn for use as a missile

A lobby card for *Legend of the Lone Ranger* (1981). Courtesy of the Paul Andrew Hutton Collection and ITC Productions.

silo, and even a fort. The pond house can't be seen from the road, but keep your eyes open for the barn and the barracks, which can be glimpsed briefly as you drive down Bonanza Creek Ranch Road.

Not far beyond Bonanza is another of the state's famed film ranches. The J. W. Eaves Ranch was built to attract Westerns to New Mexico with a convenient period backlot not far from Santa Fe. The property was partly the brainchild of writer Max Evans, who pushed the state film office to approve the construction. *The Cheyenne Social Club*, a comedy that starred Jimmy Stewart and was directed by Gene Kelly, became the first to use the backlot. When completed, the ranch included more than three dozen structures, including a church and the obligatory Western saloon.

Eaves is not currently open to the public, but you'll drive right past it on your way down Bonanza Creek Ranch Road to New Mexico State Road 14. Make a right turn there for more Western locations.

Head south until you spot the signs for Cerrillos, then make a right into the small hamlet. Park where you can on the town's small 1st Street for the shortest walking tour in this book. It'll last the length of Cerrillos's commercial center: two blocks.

Walk to the left as you entered town and stop at the intersection with Waldo Street. This two-block section of Cerrillos appeared on screen as early as 1959 when *The Magical World of Disney* visited the old mining town for an episode about the famed New Mexico lawman Elfego Baca, who made history fighting outlaws in Socorro.

Two decades later, yet another fictionalized version of a famous New Mexican visited Cerrillos and used it to stand in for yet another southern New Mexico town. This time, Cerrillos became Lincoln where Billy the Kid and his Regulators fended off rival forces.

> EXT. TUNSTALL'S STORE—LINCOLN—DAY
> A one-mile dirt road dotted with shops, a hotel, saloons. Tunstall's store, a one-story, flat-roofed trading post, is situated almost directly across the street from L. G. Murphy's "Big Store." LOCALS walk to and fro.
>
> (From the script for *Young Guns* written by John Fusco)

The crew for *Young Guns* dressed up Cerrillos's commercial district to look like Lincoln, including painting the sign for the Wortley Hotel, an actual historical inn in Lincoln. The Antonio Simoni building on the commercial side of the street still sports the faux Wortley Hotel painting as well as a "thank you" to the crew, emblazoned above a doorway.

Cross the street to Mary's Bar, which appeared in horror guru John Carpenter's *Vampires* (1998). The bar is still popular with the living, as opposed to the undead, if you want to stop for a drink.

No trip to Cerrillos is complete without a visit to The Cerrillos Turquoise Mining Museum and Casa Grande Trading Post (17 Waldo St., Los Cerrillos, NM, 87010; 505-438-3008, casagrandetradingpost.com). Part historical collection, part knick-knack store, and part petting zoo, the curio shop appeared in the Netflix show *Chambers* (2019). Created by Leah Rachel, the show explored the aftermath of a haunting heart transplant on a young woman. It starred Sivan Alyra Rose in the lead with Uma Thurman and Tony Goldwyn in supporting roles.

You can reach the trading post by heading down 1st Street and then taking a right on Waldo Street. Keep going a couple blocks to the end of town. To get to the next stop, you'll want to turn around and head back up 1st Street to Vicksville Road and make a left on County Road 59.

The Cerrillos Hills State Park Visitor Center (37 Main Street, Cerrillos, NM 87010; 505-474-0196, emnrd.nm.gov/spd/find-a-park/cerrillos-hills-state-park/) is worth a quick look if you're interested in taking a longer hike after this brief tour. The state park itself, just a few miles up the road, is home to excellent hiking trails and a number of historic mines that are partially visible from the surface. After your hike, or drink, or both, head back to New Mexico State Road 14 for the next historic Western town—Madrid is only another ten minutes heading south.

Like Cerrillos, Madrid was once the booming center of a coal-mining area. Madrid itself was created to be the ideal company town, complete with housing, recreational facilities, and a company store. The boom in coal, though, was short-lived, and vibrant Madrid faded away, eventually transforming from a buttoned-up corporate community into an off-the-grid safe haven for those seeking alternative lifestyles.

With just one major road through town, Madrid can become congested, and parking can be difficult. Find a spot where you can, and be careful walking along State Road 14, as not everyone is interested in allowing walking tours.

This tour has just two stops and can begin on either side of town. Starting from the southern end of town and walking north, the first site of interest is the Mine Shaft Tavern (2846 New Mexico State Road 14

Madrid, NM 87010; 505-473-0743, themineshafttavern.com), which is difficult to miss.

This sprawling red building is a local landmark and the center of Madrid's social life. Here, you'll find live music, food, and, of course, drinks. Built on the footprint of a bar that once served local coal miners, the Mine Shaft was constructed in 1947, but has a timeless, Western feel which makes it useful for films and television shows. Look for the Mine Shaft in *Longmire*. For a deeper exploration of the area's history (pun intended) try the attached history museum.

Continuing north, it's only a few blocks to Maggie's Diner. Currently a souvenir shop with New Mexico and movie memorabilia, Maggie's Diner has a unique distinction: the building was constructed as a temporary movie set for the buddy comedy *Wild Hogs* (2007) and later rehabbed into a permanent structure. The film starred Tim Allen, Martin Lawrence, John Travolta, and William H. Macy as the titular Wild Hogs, a weekend motorcycle troop that crosses paths with a true biker gang. On the run from their new rivals, the Wild Hogs take refuge at a diner run by a woman named Maggie (Marisa Tomei). The Hogs enjoy a chile festival in this fictionalized version of Madrid until their enemies finally arrive for the climactic showdown.

After the shoot, the production left the faux diner in place. The diner drew so much attention that entrepreneurs finally purchased it and paid for the structure to be made permanent. Inside you'll find a selection of T-shirts and souvenirs. From here, you can wrap up your Madrid walk or take some time to check out the many galleries in town.

The final stop on this tour will be on the return trip to Santa Fe, so get back in your car and head north on State Route 14 for about twenty minutes. Before the turn to 599, keep a lookout for the Old State Penitentiary, which has proved to be one of more important and versatile filming locations in the state. It's visible on your left as you drive.

In 1980 the Old State Pen was the site of a violent prison rebellion in which the inmates of the penitentiary overthrew the guards and took control of the facility. Once in control, the inmates took twelve officers hostage and

The Old Main State Penitentiary as it appears in *The Longest Yard* (2005). Courtesy of Paramount Pictures.

then tortured and killed known informants among the incarcerated. All told, they killed thirty-three inmates. Amazingly, the Old State Penitentiary stayed in operation for almost two more decades before they moved to a new facility just down the road.

Almost immediately after closing, the Old State Pen sprang back to life as a popular set for prison films. Look for it in the 2003 remake of *The Longest Yard,* starring Adam Sandler as a disgraced quarterback sentenced to hard time at a maximum security prison. The production added faux fronted towers to the cell blocks that were left in place and can still be seen.

The New Mexico Department of Corrections occasionally offers tours of the Old State Pen. Be prepared to learn about the grim history of the riot. (4311 New Mexico State Road 14, Santa Fe, NM 87502; cd.nm.gov/divisions/corrections-industries/old-main/)

From here, you can head back to central Santa Fe on I-25 or on New Mexico State Road 14.

Selected Filmography

Becker, Walt, dir. *Wild Hogs*. Buena Vista Pictures, 2007. Film.

Cain, Christopher, dir. *Young Guns*. Twentieth Century Fox, 1988. Film.

Carpenter, John, dir. *Vampires*. Columbia Pictures, 1998. Film.

Coraci, Frank, dir. *The Ridiculous 6*. Netflix Studios, 2015. Film.

D'Onofrio, Vincent, dir. *The Kid*. Lionsgate, 2019. Film.

Favreau, Jon, dir. *Cowboys & Aliens*. Universal Studios, 2011. Film.

Hill, Terence, dir. 1991; *Lucky Luke*. A-Pix Entertainment, 2000. DVD.

Hill, Terence, dir. *Botte di Natale*. Rialto Films, 1994. Film.

Kasdan, Lawrence, dir. *Silverado*. Columbia Pictures, 1985. Film.

Kelly, Gene, dir. *The Cheyenne Social Club*. National General Productions, 1970. Film.

Lester, Richard, dir. *Butch & Sundance: The Early Days*. Twentieth Century Fox, 1979. Film.

Mann, Anthony, dir. *The Man from Laramie*. Columbia Pictures, 1955. Film.

Nyby, Christian, dir. *The Magical World of Disney*. Season 5, episode 17, "Elfego Baca, Attorney at Law." Aired February 6, 1959. Walt Disney Productions, 1959. Television episode.

Rachel, Leah, creator. *Chambers*. Netflix, 2019.

Samuel, Jeymes, dir. *The Harder They Fall*. Netflix, 2021. Film.

Segal, Peter, dir. *The Longest Yard*. Paramount Pictures, 2005. Film.

Taccone, Jorma, dir. *MacGruber*. Lionsgate, 2010. Film.

Tennant, Andy, dir. *Fools Rush In*. Columbia Pictures, 1997. Film.

North of Santa Fe and Outdoor Adventure

Whatever kind of outdoor adventure you crave—it can be found within an hour or two of the Santa Fe Plaza. From hiking to skiing to rafting, it's all here, often in close vicinity to filming locations. This tour can be done as a long driving loop or a shorter out-and-back with an activity in between sections.

The first destination is a short trip directly uphill from the plaza to one of the most frequented outdoors destinations in the area. These areas shouldn't be your first destination for celeb gazing, but stars like *Longmire*'s Bailey Chase and Michael Keaton have said they spent their New Mexico downtime in the mountains near Santa Fe. Take Bishop's Lodge Road to Artist's Road and stay on it until it reaches Ski Santa Fe (New Mexico State Road 475, Santa Fe, NM 87501; 505-982-4429, skisantafe.com), where the road ends in a parking lot. There's plenty of room to park in the summer, but in the winter, expect much more congestion.

When not covered in snow, the slopes of Ski Santa Fe make excellent mountainsides for film and television. The steep slopes are visible in the Western *Hostiles* and the war memoir *Lone Survivor* (2013). For *Lone Survivor,* the crew used chair lifts to reach their shooting locations on the mountain. For one of the patrol scenes in the film, the crew traveled to the ski area boundary where they enjoyed see-forever views of the surrounding Sangre de Cristo Range. In the film, these peaks stood in for the mountains in Afghanistan. Lower down on the slopes, the production shot segments of the "tumble, tumble" action in which the small detachment of Navy SEALs is forced down the mountain by a much larger group of Taliban forces.

The mission begins atop the mountains in *Lone Survivor* (2013).
Courtesy of Universal Pictures.

In the winter, take the Tesuque Peak chairlift to the top for views similar to those seen by Mark Wahlberg, Taylor Kitsch, Ben Foster and Emile Hirsch, although most of their patrol took place out of the ski area boundaries. The best way to walk along the boundary is in the fall when the ski area operates the Super Chief Quad lift, which allows hikers to walk along the boundary and onto nearby trails, like Aspen Vista. The fall lift also provides access for mountain biking if hiking doesn't provide enough adrenaline.

That famed Aspen Vista Trail is not named idly and is more easily accessible on the way back to Santa Fe. Take Hyde Park down about two miles and you'll see the busy trailhead, especially when the leaves are in season. In the fall, the area glows yellow as the Aspen trees change color, making the trail popular with photographers. For most, the trail is a simple out-and-back that goes almost six miles to the ski area and returns along the same route. Obviously, you can make it a much shorter trip if you choose. Parking is available along the road.

The next stop on this tour may take an hour to reach from Ski Santa Fe. Start by finishing the drive down the mountain. Then, take Paseo de

An alternative route to Bandelier, albeit a longer one, is through Española, due straight north on 84. Showtime's cross-genre dark comedy *The Curse* shot all around the center of Española, including at a Subway restaurant on Riverside Drive.

New Mexico State Road 30 meets 285 in Española and continues back to 502. A few locations to note along the way: Puye Cliff Dwellings (300 New Mexico State Road 30, Los Alamos, NM 87532; 505-917-6650, puyecliffdwellings.com). These cliff dwellings, once home to Ancestral Pueblo people, have appeared in a number of films and shows including *Flap* (1970), *Hostiles*, *Cosmos: A Spacetime Odyssey* (2014), *Second Thoughts* (1983), and *American Primeval* (2025), among others.

Perhaps lesser known than Bandelier, Puye is nearly as scenic with a more intimate experience because it is Pueblo owned and operated. Tours are usually arranged through the welcome center and conducted by locals. The area has been a hotspot for tourists for decades, originally part of the Harvey Destinations program, shuttling travelers from La Fonda to Puye for an adventure. That same center has recently been restored.

In addition to the visual appeal of the cliff dwellings, the area also has running water and a pine forest, making the area handy for Westerns. Most visitors will stop at the welcome center before reaching the wooded area well down the single road into the park.

Not far from the entrance to Puye, the Black Mesa is visible from the state road. Once part of an ancient volcano, this basalt mound is sacred to the residents of Santa Clara Pueblo and not open for visitation. You can spot the distinctive geographic feature in the film *Sudan* (1945). Although it's hard to envision this part of New Mexico as a convincing replica of Africa, that's exactly what it was in this dated epic about a slave revolt.

Peralta to New Mexico 84/285 north and the Santa Fe Relief Route 599 south. Continue to the Camino La Tierra exit, head west four miles to Old Buckman Road, and stay on the rutty dirt road for an additional 7.5 miles until you reach a parking area near the mouth of the canyon.

The sheer basalt walls of Diablo Canyon are perfect for climbing—and for Westerns, which have made scenic use of the area for years. Because the canyon naturally creates a pinch point, it's perfect for a siege, shootout, or dramatic horse-riding shots. Look for the canyon in the opening minutes of the Coen Brothers' Western remix, *The Ballad of Buster Scruggs*. It also appeared in *3:10 to Yuma* (2007).

The canyon additionally pops up in the 2005 miniseries *Into the West*. The Western followed the interwoven story of two families, one white and one Native American, as the westward movement of the United States changed their lives. The show featured an extensive cast, including Wes Studi, Beau Bridges, and Tom Berenger. The miniseries, which shot at the Western ranches and in southern New Mexico, nabbed seventeen Emmy Award nominations after it aired on TNT. Santa Fe local Kirk Ellis worked on the show as a writer and supervising producer. He went on to win an Emmy for another miniseries, *John Adams*. The 2008 HBO historical drama featured Paul Giamatti in the titular role.

Diablo Canyon's rugged beauty presents some ideal climbing opportunities. The cliffs offer bolted routes that range in difficulty from 5.8 to 5.13 on the Yosemite scale. Although these are fairly straightforward climbs, they're not for the uninitiated. You'll need to bring your own equipment and a more detailed description of the routes, or hire a guide. The walking trail is much more self-explanatory. Hikers will find an easy out-and-back walk down the center of the canyon. Note that the dusty trail can be exposed and hot, so be prepared. If you're up to it, the trail goes all the way to the Rio Grande near the spot where the town of Buckman once stood alongside a river crossing. You can return along the same route.

To get to the next stop, head back to the Santa Fe Relief Route and return to 84/285 north. The road goes past a few additional film highlights

Camel Rock as it appears in *Greaser's Palace* (1975). Courtesy of Cinema5 Distributing.

on the way to Bandelier National Monument (15 Entrance Road, Los Alamos, NM 87544; 505-672-3861 x 0, nps.gov/band).

The first, on the left side as you head north, is the Santa Fe Opera (301 Opera Drive, Santa Fe, NM 87506; 505-986-5900, santafeopera.org). This open-air venue draws international talent for yearly, seasonal performances. The venue is open in the summer. Special events and concerts sometimes pop elsewhere on the calendar. Make sure to schedule plenty of time before each performance, as one of the highlights is actually in the parking lot. Many operagoers arrive early to set up elaborate tailgates before each performance. The typical menu is fit more for a five-star restaurant than a football party.

Ad for *Sudan* (1945). Courtesy of the Paul Andrew Hutton Collection and Universal Pictures.

The opera made a cameo in *Crazy Heart*. Here Jeff Bridges, playing Bad Blake, makes amends for allowing his struggles with alcoholism to endanger his friend's child. The opera provides a scenic backdrop for his heartfelt and heartstring-pulling apology.

You can also look for the opera in the romantic comedy *Tao of Steve*. Actor Donal Logue, playing the lady's man Dex, falls for Syd Goodman, who is disgusted by his tricks but forced into giving him a ride to work every day. Despite their differences, Dex wins Syd with his charms. She takes him to the opera, where she works as a set designer. Dex's backstage tour includes costumes, the set, and the main stage itself. Eventually Syd learns the truth about Dex's manipulation of women using guidelines he created by combining the cool of Steve McQueen with ancient philosophies. Afterward Dex struggles to get her back.

Continuing north, the next point of interest is the aptly named Camel Rock in Tesuque Pueblo. It's visible on the left side of the road, but there's also a vista point if you'd like to stop and a get a photograph. This odd rock formation appeared briefly in a dream sequence in Robert Downey Sr.'s *Greaser's Palace*. (During production, Downey Sr. sent his son, the actor Robert Downey Jr., to a Montessori school in Santa Fe. Years later, Downey Jr. returned to Santa Fe for the making of *Oppenheimer* and was excited to see his old stomping grounds. For more on Downey Sr., you can check out the 2022 documentary *Sr.* directed by Downey Jr.) Across from the rock formation, the old casino serves as a production facility for visiting shows and had the rare distinction of being among the studios owned and operated by a Native American tribe. It appears in the series *Dark Winds* several times. The studio is not open to the public, but the newer casino is located next to the opera and hard to miss thanks to its glass façade.

Farther north, the Pueblo of Pojoaque is worth a quick stop and was used extensively in the unaired pilot *Scalped* (2017), based on the comic of the same named created by R. M. Guera and Jason Aaron. The pilot starred Gil Birmingham as a tribal leader with a great deal of power and some possibly extra-legal sources of income. Nearby, the Poeh Museum

The Los Alamos Project main gate as it appeared in 1943. A reconstruction is still visible in Los Alamos today off New Mexico 502 at East Road on the way into town. Courtesy of Los Alamos National Laboratory. Wikimedia Commons.

(78 Cities of Gold Road, Santa Fe, NM 87506; 505-455-5041, poehcenter.org), just off the highway, was partially designed by local sculptor Roxanne Swentzell, who also has a tower gallery nearby.

Just past Pojoaque, take New Mexico State Road 502 toward Los Alamos and then to White Rock, where you'll find shuttle parking for Bandelier National Monument. It's worth devoting several hours to exploring the park, which features Native American cave dwellings built primarily between the thirteenth and sixteenth centuries by the forebears of the modern Pueblo people.

The park and its ancient architecture made an ideal location to stage a replicated snakebite ceremony for the independent hit film *Billy Jack* (1971). Featuring real dancers from Taos Pueblo, the ceremony was meant to give the film's hero, the martial arts expert *Billy Jack*, a new sense of focus in his fight to keep the reservation safe.

The scene was filmed at Tyuonyi Pueblo, which is accessible on the Pueblo Loop, a gentle 1.4-mile walk around the center of the park. The trail begins at the visitor center, where the shuttle drops you off. Walk through the small museum before you head off on the trail. Inside, a small model of Tyuonyi Pueblo gives an impression of what the large villages looked like when inhabited. Other exhibits illustrate Ancestral Pueblo life.

From the back door of the visitor center, stay on the concrete path for the Pueblo Loop. The trail winds past the Great Kiva before it makes its way to Tyuonyi Pueblo. This great village once housed more than a thousand people and stood two to three stories tall.

From the remnants of the Pueblo, the trail curves up into the soft cliffs of Frijoles Canyon. Here, the Ancestral Pueblo people carved their residences into the hardened volcanic ash called "tuff." These excavated caves, or "cavates," are accessible via a sequences of stairs and ladders placed in the cliffs.

More adventurous walkers should stay on the trail and continue past the Longhouse and back on to the main trail alongside Frijolitos Creek. The path leads to Alcove House, which is not for the faint of heart. More

Lobby card from *The Atomic City* (1952). Courtesy of the Paul Andrew Hutton Collection and Paramount Pictures.

than one hundred feet of ladders leads to the elevated alcove, where you'll find some great views of the canyon. From Alcove House, follow the river back to the visitor center.

From the shuttle stop in White Rock, there are two routes to Los Alamos: New Mexico State Road 4 follows the road back to Bandelier. New Mexico State Road 30, on the road back to Santa Fe, is equally scenic. Either way, the Atomic City is worth a visit.

Once home to an isolated Boys Camp, physicist J. Robert Oppenheimer changed the course of local and world history when he chose the site as a secret laboratory that would be used to develop atomic weaponry, code named as Project Y and then as the Manhattan Project. Almost overnight, the sleepy village became the bustling center of American nuclear science. The town, and the project, had to grow in absolute secrecy. The Americans were in a race against the Germans to develop the technology, and any stolen information could drastically have altered the competition.

The Bradbury Science Museum (1450 Central Avenue, Los Alamos, NM, 87544; 505-667-4444, lanl.gov/museum/) has an excellent rundown of the Manhattan Project, its evolution into the Los Alamos National Labs, and the multifaceted areas of research currently underway in their expansive facilities. The museum also makes a good starting point for a walking tour of Los Alamos.

On foot, you can head down Central Avenue toward the Fuller Lodge, which was built in 1928 and now serves as a local arts center. Christopher Nolan's *Oppenheimer* used the historic building for a Christmas party during which Oppenheimer receives an important bit of news from scientist Niels Bohr. Fuller Lodge also made the perfect venue for Oppenheimer to tell his team that the bomb was successfully detonated. In Nolan's hands, the scene became a grim but fantastical portrayal of Oppenheimer's fears about what he had unleashed on the world.

The film also shot in the Oppenheimer House, just up the street on Bathtub Row. Once part of the Ranch School, these homes were the only residences in the area with bathtubs during the Manhattan Project, hence the name. To shoot on Bathtub Row, the film made an arrangement with the historical society, agreeing that some of the period set dressing the production purchased would be left on site. As a result, the historical society got a head start in refurbishing the historic home.

There are more *Oppenheimer* locations nearby, including the Women's Army Corp (WAC) dormitory building one block over on 17th Street. The structure was built in 1943 to house women working on the Manhattan Project and was recently acquired by Los Alamos County to be restored and added to the national park. The old dorm spaces were converted into the labs for the production. They also turned a common room in to a lecture hall.

Nolan's film also made use of the Guaje Pines Cemetery and the nearby Dot Grant Trail, which are slightly out of walking distance on Diamond Drive. The short trail once connected local homesteads. More trails are accessible at the Pajarito Mountain Ski Area, which has also been featured on film. In winter, the ski area features forty-four trails. In summer, many of the trails and access roads are available for mountain biking. Look for segments of the mountain to appear in the fire fighter drama *Only the Brave*.

Sequences of the film *Silkwood* (1983) also shot in Los Alamos. Starring Meryl Streep, Kurt Russell, and Cher, the film delved into the life of an employee at a nuclear power plant who raises questions about safety practices, only to discover that her own life is in danger.

Get back in your car to see *Longmire*'s marquee location. The adaptation of Craig Johnson's best-selling novels made frequent trips to the Valles Caldera National Preserve (39201 New Mexico Highway 4, Jemez Springs, NM 87025; 505-670-1612, nps.gov/vall/), which is a short drive up the hill. Take New Mexico 501 to New Mexico Highway 4 toward Jemez Springs. The entrance to the national preserve will be on your right around mile marker 39.

The gentle grasslands and rolling hills of the caldera belie a violent geologic past that included the eruption of a massive volcano just over a million years ago. The ash and pyroclastic flow from the volcano eventually became the soft cliffs and canyons of the Pajarito Plateau. In the process, the mountain also destabilized and eventually collapsed creating one of

Not nearly as famous as its northern neighbor state for outdoors recreation, New Mexico offers a solid selection of skiing, hiking, biking, and climbing opportunities in addition to the ones mentioned in this tour. Here are a few of the highlights not included in, but often adjacent to, this tour.

Although it isn't the oldest of the bunch, Taos Ski Valley (116 Sutton Place, Taos Ski Valley, NM 87525; 575-776-2291, skitaos.com) is the granddaddy of New Mexico ski areas. Famous for steep slopes and a big mountain, the resort can compete with any in Colorado or Utah. Lift tickets are available individually or as part of the Ikon network of ski areas. Hotels can be found at the base of the ski area. Alternatively, the slopes are about a twenty-minute drive from greater Taos. (Other nearby skiing options include Angel Fire and Red River.) While skiing in Santa Fe is heavily dependent on fluctuating winter conditions, Taos also features a state-of-the-art snowmaking system that provides some insulation from dry winters. Fortunately, Taos is only an hour's drive from Santa Fe, making it easy to add a ski trip to a walking tour of the City Different.

The mountains by the ski valley appeared in several films, including the 2006 Western *Seraphim Falls*. Starring Pierce Brosnan and Liam Neeson, the film shot there to take advantage of the snowy conditions. During the production, director David Von Ancken joked that the film managed to work in eighty-degree weather in Lordsburg one day and twenty-degree weather in Taos the next day. The action blockbuster *Batman v. Superman: Dawn of Justice* (2015) also shot at altitude in the peaks by the ski valley. This big-budget Warner Bros. tentpole created their own village near Deming for one of the first scenes in the film.

If there are two things that New Mexico offers, they're solitude and ruggedness. Both are available in droves. Here you'll find great views, challenging ascents, and lush forests, making hiking perhaps New Mexico's best activity.

Several of the state's most marquee trails can be reached at the base of the Santa Fe Ski Basin, just minutes from the plaza. The Nambe Lake Trail, for instance, rises out of the skiing parking lot and climbs to a scenic body of water high in the mountains for a round-trip distance of about six miles. The initial ascent on that hike is on the Windsor Trail, which also heads to Lake Katherine or to Santa Fe Baldy for the truly adventurous.

If you'd rather acclimate to the Santa Fe altitude before attempting a serious trek, try the Dale Ball Trails, up Hyde Park Road en route to Ski Santa Fe. The trail system is also open to mountain bikes, although you'll have to work your way around big crowds of walkers. The Ball Trails could be a great warm-up for longer walks and hikes.

Another easy walk or bike ride through town, the Rail Trail, parallels the spur route to Lamy, for a gentler, rolling bike ride. You can ride the full fifteen miles by starting at the Rail Yard. Or you can park at the Rabbit Road trailhead, near the intersection with Vereda Serena. The dirt trail goes just over eleven miles to Lamy from that start. Check out the Page to Screen tour (page 4) for more details. For bike rentals and more options try New Mexico Bike N Sport (504 W Cordova Rd, Santa Fe, NM 87505; 505-820-0809, nmbikensport.com).

Just minutes from downtown Santa Fe, and much shorter, the Picacho Peak Trail yields sweeping views of the city after a brisk and steep hoof up a jagged hill. The parking area for this popular trail, just beyond the Randall Davey Audubon Center, fills up quickly. There's additional overflow parking down Cerro Gordo. The four-mile trail begins across the street and winds its way up the hill to a rocky summit. Mile marker posts provide frequent directions. The trail connects to the Dale Ball system, if you're interested in extending your hike.

In Albuquerque, La Luz trail, a steep climb up the side of the Sandia, ranks among the state's most famous hikes. The demanding hike ends with rewarding views of northern New Mexico. Rather than walk down, you can switch it up and take the tram as long as you've set up a shuttle and parked one car at the tram and another at the trailhead. Or you can walk from the tram parking back to the trailhead, which adds about a mile to your day.

The trail is extremely demanding, although it's not technical. Most of the seven miles are on a wide dirt path. Sections, though, cross over rock falls and can test your ankle strength, making sturdy hiking boots a necessary accessory. Even for a seasoned hiker, this can be a full day draining adventure (although the author has seen people do the hike in flip-flops).

Not known for its bodies of water, New Mexico's high desert still offers a few notable spots for river rafting and fly fishing, both within an easy drive of Santa Fe. It's best to grab a guide for these adventures, although you can go solo.

The best whitewater rafting in the state can be found along the Rio Grande on one of two stretches called the Taos Box and the Racecourse. The Box is significantly more technical of the two, usually reserved for experienced kayakers and boaters. Commercial rafters primarily run on the Racecourse, which has an assortment of class II and III rapids perfect for splashy thrills. Try New Wave Rafting Company (2110 New Mexico State Road 68, Embudo, NM, 87531; 800-984-1444, newwaverafting.com) or Santa Fe Rafting (1000 Cerrillos Rd., Santa Fe, NM 87505; 505-988-4914, santaferafting.com).

If you'd rather head to the Rio Grande Del Norte National Monument (New Mexico State Road 68, Embudo, NM, 87531; 575-751-4899), a 240,000-acre preserve on the titular river, on your own, you can wait until lower river volume later in the summer or fall. The river is usually at its highest in the early spring and summer as the snowpack in the mountains melts and drains into the Rio Grande. Try renting an inflatable kayak or getting a stand-up paddleboard to work on those core muscles.

Follow the river north to the Rio Grande Gorge Bridge, a scenic span crossing the river north of Taos. The bridge shows up in a number of films, including *Terminator: Salvation*. The distinctive high arches and deep gorge are instantly recognizable.

Fly fishing can be found a little closer to Santa Fe on the Pecos River. Public access fishing is available near Terrero. Or you can go with a guide like High Desert Angler (460 Cerrillos Rd, Santa Fe, NM 87501; 505-988-7688, highdesertangler.com) in Santa Fe. The Pecos River flows briefly through an episode of *Longmire*.

If you'd rather dangle from a line than cast one, New Mexico also has a number of opportunities for rock climbing. In addition to the routes at Diablo Canyon, other popular spots for climbing can be found near White Rock or the cliffs below the Sandia in Albuquerque. You can check out climbing gyms in Albuquerque and Santa Fe.

the world's largest calderas. Over time, the caldera's lush soil was covered with rolling grassland and trees. The residents of the nearby pueblos made seasonal hunting camp in the region to pursue elk and deer and to gather obsidian for fashioning weapons.

A short dirt road leads to the visitor center. As you enter, you'll see the husk of a cabin below a small rise on the left. The faux structure was used in the Cate Blanchett and Tommy Lee Jones Western *The Missing* (2003). The production left the cabin standing after they wrapped, and the national preserve has opted to keep it and open it for occasional tours. The entry gate is otherwise locked.

To check out the cabin and other film sites around the valley, continue down the dirt road and park at the visitor center. From the center, it's a half mile walk to the cabin. Or you can stay on the entrance road and drive. Unlike the cabin for *The Missing*, this structure was not built specifically for production. The rustic house is nestled among a small group of cabins built by ranchers in the 1910s. The ranch manager once lived in the aptly named Foreman's Cabin, which was in use from 1918 until the early 2000s before it found a new life as the fictional home of Sheriff Longmire.

A host of other Westerns also used the verdant Valles. Gregory Peck visited with a film called *Shoot Out* in 1971, produced by the team behind John Wayne's *True Grit* (1969). A decade later, Melanie Griffith and Anjelica Huston starred in the television series *Buffalo Girls* (1995), which built a faux Western town down the valley. Pieces of the Western town are still visible, but it is difficult to reach on foot and mostly deteriorated.

Selected Filmography

Arbi, Adil El and Billal Fallah, dirs. *Scalped*. WGN, 2017. TV series.

Berg, Peter, dir. *Lone Survivor*. Universal Pictures, 2013. Film.

Coen Brothers, dirs. *The Ballad of Buster Scruggs*. Netflix Studios, 2017. Film.

Cooper, Scott, dir. *Crazy Heart*. Fox Searchlight Pictures, 2009. Film.

Cooper, Scott, dir. *Hostiles*. Waypoint Entertainment, 2017. Film.

Downey, Robert, Sr., dir. *Greaser's Palace*. Cinema 5 Distributing, 1972. Film.

Druyan, Ann, creator. *Cosmos: A Spacetime Odyssey*. Fox, 2014. TV series.

Goodman, Jenniphr, dir. *Tao of Steve*. Sony Pictures Classic, 2000. Film.

Hardy, Rod, dir. *Buffalo Girls*. CBS, 1995. TF series.

Hathaway, Henry, dir. *Shoot Out*. Universal Pictures, 1971. Film.

Howard, Ron, dir. *The Missing*. Columbia Pictures, 2003. Film.

Kosinski, Joseph, dir. *Only the Brave*. Columbia Pictures, 2017. Film.

Laughlin, Tom, dir. *Billy Jack*. Warner Bros., 1971. Film.

Mangold, James, dir. *3:10 to Yuma*. Lionsgate, 2007. Film.

Nichols, Mike, dir. *Silkwood*. Twentieth Century Fox, 1983. Film.

Nolan, Christopher, dir. *Oppenheimer*. Universal Pictures, 2023. Film.

Rawlins, John, dir. *Sudan*. Universal Pictures, 1945. Film.

Reed, Carol, dir. *Flap*. Warner Bros., 1970. Film.

Turman, Lawrence, dir. *Second Thoughts*. Universal Pictures, Associated Film Distribution, 1983. Film.

TOUR 8

Las Vegas

Less celebrated than Santa Fe or Albuquerque, Las Vegas is quietly one of the most important and historical filmmaking destinations in New Mexico. A century ago, before Hollywood was fully established as the center of American film, the city hosted two working studios run by famed silent film stars. Today the city's historic plaza makes an excellent stand-in for small-town America. Look for Las Vegas's Plaza in the shows *Roswell, New Mexico, Longmire,* and *No Country for Old Men* (2007), among many others.

The raucous days in Las Vegas, though, began long before the cameras arrived. In 1879 the railroad reached Las Vegas and transformed the sleepy town into a rollicking whistle stop and the largest city in New Mexico Territory. Famed gunslingers like Billy the Kid and Doc Holliday came through town, and so did everyone else. Las Vegas grew rapidly, thanks to the railroad's effect on the local economy, which caused a boom in construction. Many of the structures from the period are still standing, and almost nine hundred have now been placed on the historic registry.

The town's character and Western charm were already in place when Romaine Fielding got his start in the silent film industry on the East Coast before moving west to chase better views and bigger action. At first, Fielding ventured to Silver City, where his brother had tipped him off on the potential for filming explosions at a mine in the area. After shooting in Silver City, Fielding relocated to Las Vegas, where he opened a studio of sorts and even renamed a hotel, The Plaza, after himself. "Hotel Romaine" housed Fielding's crew in 1913, but the painted sign is still visible today. The Plaza Hotel (230 Plaza Street, Las Vegas, NM 87701; 505-425-3591, plazahotellvnm.com) also makes a good spot for starting a walking tour of Old Town Las Vegas.

The Plaza was built in 1882 with a grand Renaissance Revival style. The building has since been refurbished and expanded in 2008. It still operates as a hotel and has a reputation among local crew members for being haunted. Tales persist of a one-time owner still keeping an eye on his property, a century after he managed the place, and of a young guest who enjoyed her stay so much that she never left. The exterior of the building appeared in the Western *The Ballad of Gregorio Cortez* (1982). Edward James Olmos starred as a farmer who crossed paths with the law through no fault of his own. His righteous struggle soon consumes much of his life.

Take a peek inside to spot the staircase featured in the action flick *No Country for Old Men*. The film is based on the novel of the same name by Cormac McCarthy. Raised in Tennessee, McCarthy began his writing career with the publication of *The Orchard Keeper* in 1965. He went on to write a dozen books and receive both a National Book Award and a Pulitzer Prize. Two of his novels were adapted to film in New Mexico, including *No Country for Old Men* and *All the Pretty Horses* (2000; more on that below). McCarthy himself relocated to Santa Fe, where he worked with the Santa Fe Institute, an interdisciplinary research center.

The Coen Brothers' adaptation of *No Country for Old Men* filmed all around the state but used Las Vegas for a pivotal foot-chase sequence. In the scene, Llewyln Moss, played by Josh Brolin, is holed up in a nondescript hotel room when Javier Bardem, as bounty hunter Anton Chigurh, tracks him down. Chigurh breaks into the room as Moss escapes quietly before the hunt continues on the street. The chase ends in one of film's great shootouts, as the two exchange fire between parked cars on a dark street. Both men escape the fray, but barely. (Much of that action was shot at nearby Douglas and Grand Avenues.)

Take a look around the historic hotel and make sure to peek around the corner to see the old "Hotel Romaine" painting. From here you can stay on foot to see the rest of Las Vegas.

Many of the historic buildings surrounding the plaza are remnants from the railroad boom of the 1880s. The Charles Ilfeld Building is a prime example of the railroad splendor. Merchants from Taos, the Ilfelds moved to Las Vegas to take advantage of the newly arrived railroad. This Italianate-style edifice became their showplace market and still provides a beautiful addition to the Plaza Hotel.

Across Hot Springs Boulevard, the Veeder Building (1815 West Plaza) was constructed in 1895 with Moorish influence and expanded a few years later. The upper floors were dedicated apartments. The lower floors were earmarked for mercantile and worked well as the exterior of the Absaroka Sheriff's office where Walt Longmire did business. The property owners conveniently left (or added) "Sheriff's Office" decals to the entry way in the middle of the building.

The Las Vegas Plaza itself was frequently featured in episodes of *Longmire*. This grassy park was one of the early features of Las Vegas when the city was created in 1835. It became the center of the village's public life. The first bandstand was erected in 1880 and was updated seven years later. The pathways were added in 1910. Walk through the plaza to Bridge Street, a frequently used filming block.

Plaza Drugs (178 Bridge Street, Las Vegas, NM 87701; 505-425-5221, plazadrugs.com), at the entrance to Bridge Street, showed up in episodes of the earth-bound drama *Roswell, New Mexico*. The production transformed the old-style drugstore into a classic eatery called the Crashdown Cafe. The restaurant's name is an homage to the alien history of Roswell, where extra-earthly creatures supposedly crash-landed in the 1950s.

Another alien-on-earth romp, *Paul* (2011), also shot on Bridge Street. Look for a chase sequence in which the street's historic buildings are clearly visible. The sci-fi farce features Seth Rogen voicing a quirky, cannabis-obsessed extraterrestrial who goes on a road trip with two superfans played by Simon Pegg and Nick Frost. The two actors gained fame together portraying similar pals in the so-called Cornetto Trilogy of *Shaun of the Dead* (2004), *Hot Fuzz* (2007), and *The World's End* (2013), all directed by Edgar Wright.

Head down Bridge Street until you feel like turning around. Pay particular attention to the First National Bank building at the beginning of

The Castañeda Hotel appearing in *Red Dawn* (1984). Courtesy of MGM/UA.

Bridge Street. Built in 1880, the Italianate structure has a handmade cornice, setting it apart from other period buildings.

Once you're back in your car, there are a few additional film landmarks worth a short drive to see. The Carnegie Library (500 National Avenue, Las Vegas, NM 87701; lasvegasnm.gov/about-9), built in 1903, was one of many libraries built with funds donated by Gilded Age tycoon Andrew Carnegie. The library was designed to resemble Thomas Jefferson's Monticello. It appears briefly in the 1984 Cold War thriller *Red Dawn*.

Set in the fictional town of Calumet, Colorado, *Red Dawn* follows a band of high school students who fight a guerrilla campaign against an invading Communist force. The band included up-and-coming stars Patrick Swayze, Charlie Sheen, and Lea Thompson.

The "Welcome to Calumet" sign painted for the film is still visible at the corner of Grand Avenue and 6th Street. Nearby, you can also live it up and spend the night in the headquarters used by the Communist Army, La Castañeda Hotel (524 Railroad Avenue, Las Vegas, NM 87701; 505-425-3591, castanedahotel.org). The hotel also appeared in the Michael Keaton and Geena Davis political comedy *Speechless* and the Matt Damon and Penelope Cruz drama *All the Pretty Horses*. The latter was an adaptation of Cormac McCarthy's 1992 novel.

Built in 1898, the heyday of the railroad era, La Castañeda was operated by the famed Fred Harvey Company. Best known for buttoned-up service in hotels and restaurants along the rail lines, the Harvey Company ushered rail and car travelers across the country for decades. All told, the Harvey Company operated eighty-four facilities throughout the West and Southwest. La Castañeda was recently remodeled and reopened as a boutique hotel with Southwestern flair.

One final relic of the railroad days, the Montezuma Castle should be on your driving tour. Now part of the Armand Hammer United World College of the American West (UWC-USA, New Mexico Route 65, Montezuma, NM, 87731; 505-454-4200, uwc-usa.org), the multi-story hotel was initially constructed in 1881 so that railroad passengers could take advantage of the nearby hot springs. That rendition of the hotel, and its subsequent reconstruction, burned down. The current version was built in 1886 and stayed in business until 1903 when it began a second life as host for the YMCA and then the church.

The sprawling hotel was the perfect setting for Gus Trikonis's 1978 horror film *The Evil* about a former doctor who purchases an old mansion to restore and then open as a rehabilitation center. The building, it turned out, hid much more than some dry rot and burst pipes. Richard Crenna, playing the film's lead, opens an underground hatch only to release a dangerous spirit.

The made-for-television biopic *Georgia O'Keeffe* and the Star Wars–obsessed geek road-trip flick *Fanboys* (2009) shot briefly at the castle as well. United World College invested millions to restore the castle and it currently houses dorms, offices and university facilities. Tours were not offered as of press time.

Selected Filmography

Coen Brothers, dir. *No Country for Old Men*. Miramax, 2007. Film.

Fielding, Romaine, dir. *The Rattlesnake: A Psychical Species*. Lubin Manufacturing, Co. 1913. Film.

MacKenzie, Carina Adly, creator. *Roswell, New Mexico*. The CW, 2019. TV series.

Milius, John, dir. *Red Dawn*. MGM/UA Entertainment Company, 1984. Film.

Mix, Tom, dir. *Local Color*. Selig Polyscope, 1915. Film.

Mottola, Greg, dir. *Paul*. Universal Pictures, 2011. Film.

Newman, Kyle, dir. *Fanboys*. Metro-Goldwyn-Mayer, Third Rail Releasing, Comedy Central, 2009. Film.

Thornton, Billy Bob, dir. *All the Pretty Horses*. Sony Pictures, 2000. Film.

Trikonis, Gus, dir. *The Evil*. New World Pictures, 1978. Film.

Young, Robert M., dir. *The Ballad of Gregorio Cortez*. Embassy Pictures, 1982. Film.

TOUR 9

Albuquerque

New Mexico's most-populated city is also its busiest production center. The Duke City is synonymous with *Breaking Bad* and *Better Call Saul,* but films like Marvel Studios' *The Avengers* and classics like *Lonely are the Brave* and *Ace in the Hole* (1951) also shot in the shadow of the Sandia Mountains.

If you've taken I-25 south from Santa Fe, those mountains make a great first stop. Take Tramway Road NE past the Sandia Resort & Casino (30 Rainbow Road, Albuquerque, NM 87113; 505-796-7500, sandiacasino.com) until it makes a sharp left turn toward the mountains. The road ends at the Sandia Peak Tramway (30 Tramway Road NE, Albuquerque, NM, 87122; 505-856-1532, sandiapeak.com).

One of the longest aerial trams in the world, the cable car glides over the Sandia foothills to the mountain's top, a distance of about 2.7 miles. The route travels close to the backdrop of the heartbreaking finale of *Lonely Are the Brave*. Based on Edward Abbey's 1956 novel, *The Brave Cowboy,* the film follows a lone cowboy searching for his place in the modernizing American West. Kirk Douglas as Jack Burns rides into the mountains where he hopes to escape the pursuing Walter Matthau as Sheriff Morey Johnson. Amongst the boulders of the foothill, Burns attempts to take cover and fight back. Unfortunately, one cowboy cannot stem the tide of civilization. Burns's attempt to live in the open range and open country comes to a grisly end between the granite rocks below the tramway.

The tramway terminal, near the Sandia Crest, will bring you close to sites used for other productions as well. The Sandia Peak Ski Area was used in the Mark Wahlberg war drama, *Lone Survivor*. Not far away, the *Breaking Bad* crew constructed a cabin where Walter White spent his exile. The cabin has since been removed.

Breaking Bad fans will want to make their next stop either of the signature restaurants from the crime drama series. Los Pollos Hermanos, the center of the drug-addled universe of the show, is actually a fast-food restaurant called Twisters Burgers and Burritos (4275 Isleta Blvd SW, Albuquerque, NM, 87105; 505-877-2727, mytwisters.com/isleta) located in the city's South Valley. The interior of the restaurant is covered in *Breaking Bad* paraphernalia. Close to downtown, the Dog House (1216 Central Avenue NW, Albuquerque, NM, 87102; 505-243-1019), went from a local frankfurter joint to an international icon when Aaron Paul's Jesse Pinkman sold meth in the restaurant's parking lot. From the Dog House, take Central Avenue directly east to downtown.

A destination for dining and nightlife, downtown also has some distinctive architecture, highlighted by the KiMo Theater (423 Central Avenue NW, Albuquerque, NM, 87102; 505-768-3522, cabq.gov/culturalservices/kimo). Built in 1927, the functional theater showcases a "Pueblo Deco" design. The aesthetic mixes Pueblo Revival with more traditional art deco. Inside, look for cattle skulls with glowing red eyes. The KiMo makes a quick cameo in season three of *Better Call Saul*. It's also a functional theater with a full slate of films and community events.

The Central Avenue corridor heading east from the KiMo is a versatile section of the city that has appeared in films and television as other metro areas like Las Vegas, Nevada, and Chicago, Illinois. Because of its urban appearance, the stretch is constantly in demand by productions and one of your best chances for seeing a television show or film in the making. You can walk to a few of the shooting destinations listed here or drive past.

Just down the street, the S. H. Kress Building (416 Central Avenue SW, Albuquerque, NM, 87102) was once a department store. Look for it in the Kevin Costner film *Swing Vote*. Then hang a right on Gold Avenue to see the Occidental Life Building (301 Gold Avenue SW, Albuquerque, NM, 87102) modeled after Venice's Palazzo Ducale and built in 1917. You can spot this building in Billy Wilder's *Ace in the Hole* or the sci-fi flick *Transcendence* (2014).

Half-sheet poster for *Ace in the Hole*, also called *The Big Carnival* (1951). Courtesy of Paramount Pictures. Wikimedia Commons.

Hop back in your car to get to the one of Albuquerque's most distinctive sites, the Rail Yards (777 1st Street SW, Albuquerque, NM 87102). These gigantic brick and colored glass buildings have appeared in numerous films and television shows. The cavernous interiors are visible in Marvel Studios' *The Avengers*, subbing in for a New York City viaduct. The superhero film also used the exteriors of the building, as has *Breaking Bad* and the Gerard Butler film *Gamer* (2009). The Rail Yards is open for seasonal markets and events. Check out the attached Wheels Museum (1100 2nd Street SW, Albuquerque, NM, 87102; 505-243-6269, wheelsmuseum.org) for some artifacts from the building's history.

Selected Filmography

Gilligan, Vince, creator. *Breaking Bad*. American Movie Classics, 2008–2013. TV series.

Gilligan, Vince, and Peter Gould, creators. *Better Call Saul*. American Movie Classics (AMC), 2015–2022. TV series.

Miller, David, dir. *Lonely Are the Brave*. Universal Studios, 1962. Film.

Neveldine, Mark, and Brian Taylor, dirs. *Gamer*. Lionsgate, Lakeshore Entertainment, 2009.

Pfister, Wally, dir. *Transcendence*. Alcon Entertainment, Warner Bros., 2014. Film.

Stern, Joshua Michael, creator. *Swing Vote*. Walt Disney Studios Motion Pictures, 2008. Film.

Whedon, Joss, dir. Marvel Studios' *The Avengers*. Paramount Pictures, 2012.

Wilder, Billy, dir. *Ace in the Hole*. Paramount Pictures, 1951. Film.

Lobby card for *Hollywood or Bust* (1956). Courtesy of the Paul Andrew Hutton Collection and Paramount Pictures.

Acknowledgments

This book would not exist were it not for the guidance of Sonia Dickey, who came up with the idea and then helped me find the right form for it. We previously collaborated on a guide to filming throughout the state.

As always, I want to thank my family, who encouraged me throughout the process and offered helpful suggestions and additional research when I got stuck.

Thanks go also to my film family, who provided helpful tidbits. In particular, I'd like to shout out Aimee Macpherson, Kirt Bozeman, Agathe Loison-Balac, Peter McGrew, Corrine Butler, Britney Erickson, Andrés Rivas, Chance Romero, Leslie Coogan, Eames Hawker, Mark Hawker, Ashley Watson, Liz Cooke, Laura Dimauro, Jeff Wang, Tantri Wija, Morgan Demers, Candolin Cook, Devan Cook, Mari Kempes, and the late Derek Chavez. Film publicist, writer and editor Wolf Schneider shepherded along several drafts of this book. Distinguished Professor of History Emeritus Paul Andrew Hutton loaned me part of his expansive film collection, which was instrumental in writing and illustrating the book.

Jennifer Labar-Tapia at the Santa Fe Film Office was kind enough to spend hours with me going over locations in the City Different. As this book nears press, the City Different is humming with productions, and Ms. Labar-Tapia's time is much appreciated.

Finally, thanks to my grandmother Esther Morris, who fostered in me a keen sense of all things past and prologue.

Filmography

Arthur, Karen, dir. *The Staircase*. CBS, 1998. TV movie.

Balaban, Bob, dir. *Georgia O'Keeffe*. Sony Pictures Television, 2009. TV movie.

Baldwin, Hunt, and John Coveny, creators. *Longmire*. A+E Networks, 2012–2017. TV series.

Berg, Peter, dir. *Lone Survivor*. Universal Pictures, 2013. Film.

Branagh, Kenneth, dir. *Thor*. Paramount Pictures, 2011. Film.

Cain, Christopher, dir. *Young Guns*. Twentieth Century Fox, 1988. Film.

Carpenter, John, dir. *Ghosts of Mars*. Screen Gems, 2001. Film.

Carpenter, John, dir. *Vampires*. Columbia Pictures, 1998. Film.

Coen Brothers, dirs. *The Ballad of Buster Scruggs*. USA: Netflix Studios, 2017. Film.

Coen Brothers, dirs. *No Country for Old Men*. USA: Miramax, 2007. Film.

Coen Brothers, dirs. *True Grit*. USA: Paramount Pictures, 2010. Film.

Columbus, Chris, dir. *RENT*. Columbia Pictures, 2005. Film.

Conrad, Steve, and Bruce Terris, creators. *Perpetual Grace, LTD*. MGM Television, 2019–2020. TV series.

Cooper, Scott, dir. *Crazy Heart*. Fox Searchlight Pictures, 2009. Film.

Cooper, Scott, dir. *Hostiles*. Waypoint Entertainment, 2017. Film.

Coraci, Frank, dir. *The Ridiculous 6*. Netflix Studios, 2015. Film.

Donaldson, Roger, dir. *White Sands*. Warner Bros., 1992. Film.

Dowdle, John Eric and Drew, creators. *Waco*. Paramount Network, 2018. TV series.

Dowdle, John Eric and Drew, creators. *Waco: The Aftermath*. Showtime Network, 2023. TV series.

Downey, Robert, Sr., dir. *Greaser's Palace*. Cinema 5 Distributing, 1972. Film.

Druyan, Ann, creator. *Cosmos: A Spacetime Odyssey*. Fox, 2014. TV series.

Ellis, Kirk, producer. *Into the West*. TNT/Dreamworks Television, 2005. TV series.

English, John, dir. *Sons of New Mexico*. Columbia Pictures, 1949. Film.

Evans, Justin Eugene, dir. *A Lonely Place for Dying*. Humble Magi, 2009. Film.

Ficarra, Glenn, and John Requa, dirs. *Whiskey Tango Foxtrot*. Paramount Pictures, 2016. Film.

Fielder, Nathan, and Benny Safdie, creators. *The Curse*. Showtime, 2023. TV series.

Foster, Lewis, dir. *El Paso*. Paramount Pictures, 1949. Film.

Franklin, Carl, dir. *Bless Me, Ultima*. Arenas Entertainment, 2012. Film.

Frears, Stephen, dir. *The Hi-Lo Country*. Gramercy Pictures, 1998. Film.

Gilligan, Vince, creator. *Breaking Bad*. American Movie Classics (AMC), 2008–2013. TV series.

Gilligan, Vince, and Peter Gould, creators. *Better Call Saul*. American Movie Classics (AMC), 2015–2022. TV series.

Glazer, Mitch, dir. *Passion Play*. Image Entertainment, 2010. Film.

Goldstone, James, dir. *Red Sky at Morning*. Universal Pictures, 1971. Film.

Greengrass, Paul, dir. *News of the World*. Universal Pictures, 2020. Film.

Harris, Ed, dir. *Appaloosa*. Warner Brothers, 2008. Film.

Hellman, Monte, dir. *Two-Lane Blacktop*. Universal Pictures, 1971. DVD.

Hill, Terence, dir. 1991; *Lucky Luke*. A-Pix Entertainment, 2000. DVD.

Hill, Terence, dir. *Botte di Natale*. Italy: Rialto Films, 1994. Film.

Hoffman, Michael, dir. *Gambit*. CBS Films, 2012. Film.

Hopper, Dennis, and Peter Fonda, dirs. *Easy Rider*. Columbia Pictures, 1969. DVD.

Howard, Ron, dir. *The Missing*. Columbia Pictures, 2003. Film.

Iñárritu, Alejandro G., dir. *21 Grams*. Focus Features, 2003. Film.

Johnson, Lamont, dir. *A Gunfight*. Paramount Pictures, 1971. Film.

Jones, Tommy Lee, dir. *The Homesman*. Roadside Attractions, Saban Films, 2014. Film.

Kasdan, Lawrence, dir. *Silverado*. Columbia Pictures, 1985. Film.

Kasdan, Lawrence, dir. *Wyatt Earp*. Warner Bros., 1994. Film.

Kennedy, Burt, dir. *The Good Guys and the Bad Guys*. Warner Bros., Seven Arts, 1969. Film.

Kosinski, Joseph, dir. *Only the Brave*. Columbia Pictures, 2017. Film.

Laughlin, Tom, dir. *Billy Jack*. Warner Bros., 1971. Film.

Leonard, Herbert and Stirling Siliphant, creators. *Route 66*. CBS, 1960–1964. TV series.

Lester, Richard, dir. *Butch & Sundance: The Early Days*. Twentieth Century Fox, 1979. Film.

Lupino, Ida. *The Trouble with Angels*. Columbia Pictures, 1966. Film.

Lupino, Ida . *Where Angels Go, Trouble Follows*. Columbia Pictures, 1968. Film.

MacKenzie, Carina Adly, creator. *Roswell, New Mexico*. The CW, 2019. TV series.

Mangold, James, dir. *3:10 to Yuma*. Lionsgate, 2007. Film.

Maples, David, creator. *In Plain Sight*. USA Network, 2008–2012. TV series.

Marshall, George, dir. *Fancy Pants*. Paramount Pictures, 1950. Film.

Marshall, George, dir. *Valley of the Sun*. RKO Radio Pictures, 1942. Film.

McFarlane, Seth, dir. *A Million Ways to Die in the West*. Universal Pictures, 2014. Film.

Medak, Peter, dir. *Pontiac Moon*. Paramount Pictures, 1994. Film.

Mendes, Sam, dir. *Jarhead*. Universal Pictures, 2005. Film.

Miller, David, dir. *Lonely Are the Brave*. Universal Studios, 1962. Film.

Montgomery, Robert, dir. *Ride the Pink Horse*. Universal Pictures, 1947. Film.

Mottola, Greg, dir. *Paul*. Universal Pictures, 2011. Film.

Newman, Kyle, dir. *Fanboys*. Metro-Goldwyn-Mayer, Third Rail Releasing, Comedy Central, 2009. Film.

Nirmalakhandan, Rajeev, dir. *Odd Way Home*. Breaking Glass Pictures, 2014. Film.

O'Connor, Gavin, dir. *Jane Got a Gun*. The Weinstein Company, 2015. Film.

Peckinpah, Sam, dir. *Convoy*. United Artists, 1978. Film.

Phillips, Todd, dir. *Due Date*. Warner Bros., 2010. Film.

Pillsbury, Sam, dir. *Into the Badlands*. USA Network, 1991. Film.

Polish, Michael, dir. *The Astronaut Farmer*. Warner Bros., 2006. Film.

Rachel, Leah, creator. *Chambers*. Netflix, 2019.

Ramis, Harold, dir. *Year One*. Columbia Pictures, 2009. Film.

Range, Gabriel, dir. *Outlaw Prophet: Warren Jeffs*. Lifetime Television, 2014. TV movie.

Rawlins, John, dir. *Sudan*. Universal Pictures, 1945. Film.

Redford, Robert, dir. *The Milagro Beanfield War*. Universal Pictures, 1988. Film.

Reed, Carol, dir. *Flap*. Warner Bros., 1970. Film.

Reeves, Matt, dir. *Let Me In*. Overture Films, Relativity Media, 2010. Film.

Reitman, Ivan, dir. *Twins*. Universal Pictures, 1988. Film.

Roach, Jay, dir. *Game Change*. HBO Films, 2012. Film.

Roland, Graham, creator. *Dark Winds*. AMC, 2022. TV series.

Rosenberg, Stuart, dir. *Pocket Money*. First Artists, 1972. Film.

Rydell, Mark, dir. *The Cowboys*. Warner Bros., 1972. Film.

Samuel, Jeymes, dir. *The Harder They Fall*. Netflix, 2021. Film.

Segal, Peter, dir. *The Longest Yard*. Paramount Pictures, 2005. Film.

Shaw, Sam, creator. *Manhattan*. WGN America, 2014–2015. TV series.

Sheridan, Jim, dir. *Brothers*. Lionsgate, 2009. Film.

Snyder, Zack, dir. *Batman v Superman: Dawn of Justice*. USA: Warner Bros., 2016. Film.

Sommers, Stephen, dir. *Odd Thomas*. Image Entertainment, 2013. Film.

Sourya, Mouly, dir. *Trigger Warning*. Netflix, 2024. Film.

Stern, Joshua Michael, creator. *Graves*. Epix, 2016–2017. TV series.

Stewart, Scott, dir. *Legion*. Screen Gems, 2010. Film.

Tashlin, Frank, dir. *Hollywood or Bust*. Paramount, 1956. Film.

Tennant, Andy, dir. *Fools Rush In*. Columbia Pictures, 1997. Film.

Thornton, Billy Bob, dir. *All the Pretty Horses*. Sony Pictures, 2000. Film.

Trikonis, Gus, dir. *The Evil*. New World Pictures, 1978. Film.

Turman, Lawrence, dir. *Second Thoughts*. Universal Pictures, Associated Film Distribution, 1983. Film.

Underwood, Ron, dir. *Speechless*. Metro-Goldwyn-Mayer (MGM), 1994. Film.

Underwood, Ron, dir. *City Slickers*. Columbia Pictures, 1991. Film.

Van Ancken, David. *Seraphim Falls*. Samuel Goldwyn Films, 2006. Film.

Vidor, King, dir. *The Texas Rangers*. Paramount Pictures, 1936. Film.
Wacks, Jonathan, dir. *Powwow Highway*. Warner Bros., 1989. Film.
Watkins, Brian, creator. *Outer Range*. Amazon Studios, 2022. TV series.
Waugh, Ric Roman, dir. *Shot Caller*. Saban Films, 2017. Film.
Wibberley, Cormac and Marianne, creators. *National Treasure: Edge of History*. Disney+, 2023. Television.

Further Reading

Allen, Rodney William, ed. *The Coen Brothers Interviews*. University Press of Mississippi, 2006.

American Film Institute, pub. "Butch and Sundance: The Early Days (1979)." *AFI Catalog of Feature Films, the First 100 Years 1893–1993*, [2019]. http://catalog.afi.com/Catalog/MovieDetails/56140.

Armijo, John Raymond, ed. *Movies Made in New Mexico, 1898-1999*. New Mexico Film Office, New Mexico Economic Development Department, 1999.

Armijo, John Raymond, ed. "Early Filmmaking in Meadow City." New Mexico Film Office, New Mexico Economic Development Department, undated.

Basinger, Jeanine. *Silent Stars*. Alfred A. Knopf, 1999.

Berg, Jeff. *Historic Movie Theatres of New Mexico*. The History Press, 2018.

Berg, Jeff. *New Mexico Filmmaking*. The History Press, 2015.

Bernstein, Abbie. "Roswell, New Mexico: Co-showrunner Christopher Hollier chats Season 2 – Exclusive Interview." AssignmentX. March 30, 2020. assignmentx.com/2020/roswell-new-mexico-co-show-runner-christopher-hollier-chats-season-2-exclusive-interview/.

Boggs, Johnny D. *Billy the Kid on Film, 1911–2012*. McFarland, 2013.

Bowman, Jon, ed. *100 Years of Filmmaking in New Mexico*. New Mexico Department of Tourism, 1998.

Cather, Willa. *Death Comes for the Archbishop*. Vintage Books, 1990.

Gaberscek, Carlo, and Kenny Stier. *In Search of Western Movie Sites*. Jerry Schneider Enterprises, LLC., 2014.

Gomez, Adrian. "'Amazing variety': Santa Fe area doubles for 19th century Texas on 'News of the World.'" *Albuquerque Journal*, January 15, 2021.

Merron, Jeff. "Real vs. Reel: The Longest Yard." *ESPN.com*, June 6, 2005. http://www.espn.com/espn/page2/story?page=merron/050613.

Movie Locations of the Great Southwest. movies.nm-unlimited2.net

Movie-locations.com

Murray, John A. *Cinema Southwest: An Illustrated Guide to the Movies and Their Locations*. Northland Publishing, 2000.

Nemiroff, Peter. "Peter Berg and Marcus Luttrell Talk LONE SURVIVOR, Cast and Crew Dedication, Making the Movie for the Right Reasons, Honoring Lives Lost, and More." *Collider*, December 19, 2013.

Nichols, John. *Dancing on the Stones: Selected Essays*. University of New Mexico Press, 2000.

The Public Library, Albuquerque and Bernalillo County. "Filmed in New Mexico." abqlibrary.org/filmedinnm.

Radish, Christina. "Robert Taylor Talks *Longmire* and How the Show Convinced Him to Do American TV." *Collider*, June 1, 2012.

Radish, Christina. "'*Perpetual Grace, LTD*': Sir Ben Kingsley, Co-Stars and Co-Creators on Finding the Mood of the Series." *Collider*, July 9, 2019.

Schicken, Richard. *Clint Eastwood: A Biography*. Vintage Books, 1997.

Seals, David. *The Powwow Highway: A Novel*. University of New Mexico Press, 2014.

Stupfel, JP. "New Sheriff in Town." *Santa Fe Reporter*, May 27, 2014.

Weintraub, Steve. "Joel and Ethan Coen Interview – NO COUNTRY FOR OLD MEN." *Collider*, November 12, 2007.

Winkler, Peter. *Dennis Hopper: The Wild Ride of a Hollywood Rebel*. Barricade Books, 2011.

Yuan, Jada. *Unleashing Oppenheimer: Inside Christopher Nolan's Explosive Atomic-Age Thriller*. Insight Editions, 2023.